ings of the most important poems, including "The Comedian as the Letter C," "Peter Quince at the Clavier," and "Sunday Morning."

Observing that the sun—"the ideal/Of this invention, this invented world/The inconceivable idea"—dominated or played a key role in more than a third of all the poems, Mr. Morse also stresses the recurrence and importance of art, the routine and quotidian, and nature throughout the work; and he finds in the greatest poems a melding, at least momentary, of the counterforces of imagination and reality that were so consistently the matter and motive of Stevens' art.

WALLACE STEVENS
POETRY AS LIFE

WALLACE STEVENS

POETRY AS LIFE

BY SAMUEL FRENCH MORSE

PEGASUS   NEW YORK

Wallace Stevens is part of a series, Pegasus American Authors, prepared under the General Editorship of Richard M. Ludwig, Princeton University.

This endlessly elaborating poem
Displays the theory of poetry,
As the life of poetry. A more severe,

More harassing master would extemporize
Subtler, more urgent proof that the theory
Of poetry is the theory of life,

As it is, in the intricate evasions of as,
In things seen and unseen, created from nothingness,
The heavens, the hells, the worlds, the longed-for lands.

❖ ❖ ❖ ❖ ❖ ❖ ❖ ❖ ❖ ❖ ❖ ❖ ❖ ❖ ❖ ❖ ❖ ❖ ❖

It is not in the premise that reality
Is a solid. It may be a shade that traverses
A dust, a force that traverses a shade.

"An Ordinary Evening in New Haven," xxviii, xxxi

FOREWORD

No BIOGRAPHY of Wallace Stevens yet exists; and from the point of view of some of his admirers, none is necessary. The poems, they say, are the life, or all of the life that matters, as if, somehow, they had no context at all or their individuality could be wholly divorced from the context out of which they grew. Other readers have assumed that as a poet of ideas, he spent a lifetime reading philosophy and restating what he had absorbed in images and symbols; and the assurance with which his "debt" to philosophers and other poets has been asserted often leaves one wondering what Stevens had of his own.

It is certainly true that the lives of few other writers can have been less adventurous or more self-contained; and despite the publication of nearly nine hundred letters and journal excerpts from a still undetermined total that far exceeds three thousand, the legend of inaccessibility, mystery, and uncommunicativeness which surrounded him for so long persists. The details of the early years are still to be filled in, although his childhood, his undergraduate career at Harvard, and his life as a law student lacked the glamor that is conventionally associated with the figure of the young poet; and even during the last years, when fame had overtaken him, his was at best "a private face" in any "public place" he visited.

But unless one subscribes wholeheartedly to the notion that

the character of a poet's work is wholly separable from the kind of life he actually lived, or that what a poet has to say about his work is not germane to it, the attempt to bring the life and the poetry into relationship has to be made. What Stevens had to say to Hi Simons (whose unfinished book might have become the book on Stevens that is still to be written) is clearly to the point:

> Obviously, it is not possible to tell what one's own poems mean, or were intended to mean. On the other hand, it is not the simplest thing in the world to explain a poem. I thought of it this way this morning: a poem is like a man walking on the bank of a river, whose shadow is reflected in the water. If you explain a poem, you are quite likely to do it either in terms of the man or in terms of the whole. When I said recently that a poem was what was on the page, it seems to me now that I was wrong because that is explaining in terms of the man. But the thing and its double always go together.

And in another letter, a little later, he said: "The man, the poet, by synecdoche becomes poetry." Yet he also wrote:

> A critic would never be free to speak his own mind if it was permissible for the poet to say that he intended something else. A poet, or any writer, must be held to what he puts down on the page. This does not mean that, if the critic happens to know the intention of the poet, it is not legitimate for him to make use of it, but it does mean that, if he does not happen to know, it is not of the slightest consequence that he should know, even if what he says the poem means is just the reverse of what the poet intended it to mean. The basis of criticism is the work, not the hidden intention of the writer.

It would be difficult to disagree with any of these statements. They do not cancel each other out; they merely sug-

gest that for Stevens what he had to say on this particular
issue, as on many other issues, was

> an and yet, and yet, and yet—
> As part of the never-ending meditation . . .

and the life of his mind. It seemed, then, that a book which
tried to bring into focus some of the apparent contradictions
and inconsistencies, as well as the steadfast convictions he
expressed in both his life and his work, would be of value
to the reader attracted to the poetry and interested in knowing something about the poet himself. Rereading the poems,
the letters, and much criticism has only reconfirmed the
belief, as Stevens put it, that "one must stand by one's own
ideas, or not at all." It has also led me to the conclusion
that although there are many ways to approach his work, the
greatest difficulty it presents involves tone—the attitude that
the writer wants the reader to take toward the poetry. He
himself said that no one could be more serious about poetry;
but because "one's sense of humor is the clue to the most
serious part of one's nature," it is not always easy to catch
the inflections of feeling that are always modifying the literal
sense of the poems. To read *Parts of a World* as satire, he
warned an old friend, was to misread the book; but to read
it as an exercise in aesthetic theory would be equally wrong.
When at the end of "Notes toward a Supreme Fiction," he
addresses the world, he does so in the voice of a lover, sophisticated, interested as much in his own emotions as he is
in his beloved, a little distant, but with the greatest of respect:

> Fat girl, terrestrial, my summer, my night,
> How is it I find you in difference, see you there
> In a moving contour, a change not quite completed?
>
> You are familar yet an aberration.
> Civil, madam, I am, but underneath
> A tree, this unprovoked sensation requires

That I should name you flatly, waste no words,
Check your evasions, hold you to yourself.
Even so when I think of you as strong or tired,

Bent over work, anxious, content, alone,
You remain the more than natural figure. You
Become the soft-footed phantom, the irrational

Distortion, however fragrant, however dear.
That's it: the more than rational distortion,
The fiction that results from feeling. Yes, that.

They will get it straight one day at the Sorbonne.
We shall return at twilight from the lecture
Pleased that the irrational is rational,

Until flicked by feeling, in a gildered street,
I call you by name, my green, my fluent mundo.
You will have stopped revolving except in crystal.

The feeling evoked by such poetry is no less feeling for having been contained; and if it is mental rather than sensuous,
discreet rather than unchecked, it still has its power. Nothing
could be more fatal to poetry of this sort than to abstract its
"meaning" from the feeling aroused by the very language in
which it is expressed. "There is no wing like meaning,"
Stevens said in the "Adagia"; and, as if to fix the thing he
was trying to get at more precisely, he reiterated the metaphor again and again: "There must be some wing on which
to fly"; "A poem is a pheasant"; "Poetry is a pheasant dis-
appearing in the brush." But the meaning, as in any true
metaphor, was that which does not exist without its words;
the "thing said" was also "the language used in saying it,"
poetry both as his sense of life and as an artifact, the thing
itself and the thing it represented. It is no wonder that he
believed "the reading of a poem should be an experience,"
like "experiencing an act," and that "its writing must be all
the more so."

The extraordinarily high value he put upon poetry, like the glorification of the role of the poet such a value implies, may thus in part account for his egotism and for his conviction that any poet inevitably writes for an elite. He sometimes went so far as to say, "One does not write for any reader except one." Having abandoned a belief in God, or at least living in an age which had abandoned its traditional beliefs, he turned to poetry as "a means of redemption." One no longer wrote to the greater glory of God, but to the glory of man and his world, and for whoever believed such glory was possible, even though the audience might be limited to one. As early as 1899, he found in the "Preface" to Santayana's *Interpretations of Poetry and Religion* a precedent, at least, for assuming the role of poet in preference to that of priest or philosopher. Religion's function, Santayana says, is "to draw from reality materials for the image of the ideal to which reality ought to conform, and to make us citizens, by anticipation, in the world we crave." In a world in which religion has failed, and which is "all of paradise that we shall know," the role of the poet is to celebrate the possible, perhaps even the present, perfecting of earth. This task falls to the poet rather than to the philosopher, Santayana says, because the "preoccupations of a hungry and abstract fanaticism poison the liberty nominally allowed [the imagination], bias all vision, and turn philosophy which should be the purest of delights into an obsession and a burden to the soul."

But it is the eloquent paean to the imagination itself in the opening chapter of *Poetry and Religion,* which furnishes the great analogues with Stevens's thought and poetry, from "Sunday Morning" to "The Hermitage at the Center," "Prologues to What Is Possible," "A Quiet Normal Life," and "To an Old Philosopher in Rome," in which the acknowledgment of his abiding affection for the "superb figure" of Santayana is most movingly expressed. In a proliferation that is almost uncanny, the figures from Santayana's book reappear in the poetry, the essays, and the "Adagia," sometimes metamorphosed almost beyond recognition, sometimes unaltered, but always in a context which makes them Stevens's own. It may also be that, having found so much to agree with in *Poetry and Religion,* Stevens found the justification for his role as poet in a challenge to his own deepest convictions; for Santayana also said,

> The vividness and persistence of the figures of many of the gods came from the fact that they were associated with institutions and practices which controlled the conception of them and kept it young. The fictions of a poet, whatever his genius, do not produce illusion because they do not attach themselves to realities in the world of action. They have character without power and names without local habitations. The gods in the beginning had both. Their image, their haunts, the reports of their apparitions and miracles, gave a nucleus of empirical reality to the accretions of legend.

For Stevens, however, although "reality" was "only the base," it was the "base" for all poetry; and if his fictions did not "attach themselves to realities in the world of action," the practical world of making a living, they never deserted the world of nature or the inner world in which he lived—"the hermitage at the center," which is, after all, as real as any other world.

He was as scrupulous in the payment of his intellectual and artistic debts as he was in the payment of his debts in "the world of action." After acknowledging his debt to others —to Santayana, to Bergson and Pater, to Henri Focillon, or, as some would have it, to Mallarmé, Valéry, Wittgenstein, Schopenhauer, and Nietzsche—one must acknowledge the debt to his own originality, which is, after all, what makes him the great figure he is.

Hancock Point, Maine, 1969   S.F.M.

ACKNOWLEDGMENTS

My greatest acknowledgment must be to the American Council of Learned Societies for a fellowship which enabled me to undertake the research for the present volume. I must also thank Northeastern University for the sabbatical leave which has made its completion possible.

Without the *Letters,* selected and edited by Holly Stevens, no new book on Stevens can be written; at every turn, it provides insights into and confirmation of the background and nature of his poetry and thought. But no single book, new or old, can exhaust the possibilities of fruitful investigation, in any case; and that, after all, is as it should be, if only because the comity of scholarship requires it.

The following poems quoted in full from the works of Wallace Stevens are used by permission of Alfred A. Knopf:

Dedicatory poem, III x, and Epilogue to "Notes toward a Supreme Fiction," "The Man with the Blue Guitar XV," "Anecdote of the Jar," "Autumn Refrain," "Tea at the Palaz of Hoon," "The Man Whose Pharynx Was Bad," "Theory," "Six Significant Landscapes VI," "The Virgin Carrying a Lantern," "Anecdote of the Abnormal," "Man and Bottle," "The Indigo Glass in the Grass," "Metaphors of a Magnifico," "A Completely New Set of Objects," "The Poem That Took the Place of a Mountain," and "As You Leave the Room."

The following poems are cited in excerpts:

"An Ordinary Evening in New Haven" (19 lines); "Academic

Discourse at Havana" (20 lines); "The Latest Freed Man" (4 lines); "Study of Two Pears" (5 lines); "The Poems of Our Climate" (10 lines); "Connoisseur of Chaos" (6 lines); "The Snow Man" (3 lines); "The Common Life" (3 lines); "The Ordinary Women" (12 lines); "The Comedian as the Letter C" (52 lines); "Notes toward a Supreme Fiction" (43 lines); "The Idea of Order at Key West" (13 lines); "The Man on the Dump" (6 lines); "A Primitive Like an Orb" (18 lines); "Bouquet of Roses in Sunlight" (3 lines); "Long and Sluggish Lines" (5 lines); "Not Ideas about the Thing but the Thing Itself" (5 lines); "To an Old Philosopher in Rome" (6 lines); "Nomad Exquisite" (8 lines); "Bantams in Pine-Woods" (5 lines); "The Weeping Burgher" (6 lines); "O Florida, Venereal Soil" (10 lines); "Cy Est Pourtraicte, Madame Ste Ursule et Les Unze Mille Vierges" (5 lines); "Disillusionment of Ten O'Clock" (4 lines); "Earthy Anecdote" (5 lines); "Peter Quince at the Clavier" (16 lines); "Botanist on Alp, No. 1" (7 lines); "Owl's Clover" (22 lines); "Three Travelers Watch a Sunrise" (8 lines).

"Colors" is quoted from *Wallace Stevens, The Making of Harmonium*, by Robert Buttel, Princeton University Press (part of the "unpublished material copyrighted by Holly Stevens").

The following prose works by Wallace Stevens are used by permission of Alfred A. Knopf:

Passages from "The Noble Rider and the Sound of Words" and "Effects of Analogy," from *The Necessary Angel*.

Passages from "The Irrational Element in Poetry," "The Whole Man: Perspectives, Horizons," "Preface to *Time of Year*," "John Crowe Ransom: Tennessean," and "Adagia," from *Opus Posthumous*.

Dust-jacket statement from *Ideas of Order*.

Unpublished letters of Wallace Stevens to Thomas Lea and Oscar Williams are used in part, with permission of Holly Stevens. (The letter to Oscar Williams was used in my essay, "Wallace Stevens, Bergson, Pater," in ELH, reprinted in *The Act of the Mind*). Passages (about 10 lines) from "Bowl,

Cat and Broomstick," material from notebooks cited in "Wallace Stevens, Bergson, Pater," and the Introduction to *Opus Posthumous,* are used by permission of Holly Stevens and Alfred A. Knopf.

Passages from the *Letters of Wallace Stevens* (about 650 lines) are used by permission of Holly Stevens and Alfred A. Knopf.

For quotations from *The Dyer's Hand* and *The Double Man,* by W. H. Auden, permission comes from Random House. Randall Jarrell's review of the *Collected Poems* was published in the *Yale Review.* Stevens's answers to an inquiry are from *Partisan Review,* Summer 1939.

CONTENTS

WALLACE STEVENS

POETRY AS LIFE 🔲

PROEM

"I HAVE no life," Wallace Stevens once complained to himself, "except in poetry"; to which he added, with characteristic nicety and self-possession, "No doubt that would be true
if my whole life was free for poetry." Like other statements
he made about the relation of life to art and of his own life
to his own art, this one has its ambiguities, as the two quite
different meanings it gives to "life" make clear. Ambiguity
aside, however, it echoes the conviction of Henry James that
"It is art that *makes* life, makes interest, makes importance
. . . and I know of no substitute whatever for the force and
beauty of its process." But Stevens in some ways seems to
have gone even farther than James in equating life with art.
For him art was, "broadly, the form of life or the sound or
color of life," and "considered as form (in the abstract)" it
was "often indistinguishable from life itself." Thus poetry
could mean those intervals when simply to be and to enjoy
being provided all the satisfactions necessary to make life
"complete in itself": it created, by imaginative "extensions
of reality," "a fictitious existence on an exquisite plane,"
which, however impermanent it might be, gave life its greatest sanction. The poems which "got themselves written down"
and published were in a sense illustrations or records of such
moments, or of the desire to achieve such moments; and yet
it was not, he said in 1955, "what I have written but what I

should like to have written that constitutes my true poems,
the uncollected poems which I have not had the strength to
realize." The modesty with which he summed up his achievement ironically underscored his ambitions not only for poetry
and life but also for poetry as life and life as poetry.

He would have liked the poems to stand as his true biography. It may be that his ambitions for poetry and especially
for his own poetry made him unusually jealous of his privacy,
not only because business limited the amount of time he
could give to poetry but also because the literary life seemed
to him suspect. To an old friend who had written to con-
gratulate him on winning the *Nation*'s poetry prize in 1936,
he protested against a notice (which he had not seen) of the
award in a local newspaper as "terribly cheap limelight,"
assuming with some justification that it would make a good
deal of the apparent incongruity of a lawyer's being a poet
and little or nothing of his poem. To most questions about
himself, his family, and his background, he seldom replied at
all until the last twenty years of his life; and even in his
report for the fiftieth anniversary of his class at Harvard he
stated merely that his occupation was "vice-president, Hartford Accident & Indemnity Company," although he regarded
the honorary degree Harvard conferred on him that year in
recognition of his accomplishments as a poet as "the highest
prize" he could ever win.

He believed that poetry itself was "not personal"—not,
that is, a means of public self-aggrandizement. But it had
everything to do with the self, as even a casual acquaintance
with the poems makes evident. What he meant is partly
summed up in two characteristic statements. The first is from
a notebook in which he wrote down passages he had come
across in his reading; in this instance, part of an article by
Graham Bell on an exhibition of Cézannes. The article was
noteworthy, Stevens said, "both for itself and because it adds
to subject and manner the thing that is incessantly overlooked:
the artist, the presence of the determining personality. Without that reality no amount of other things matters much."

The other is from a letter to Barbara Church, in which he described his pleasure in an exhibition of Dufys: "When I was able to sit in a room full of the paintings . . . my chief pleasure was the companionship of Dufy himself, without any factitious chic."

To such observations, many of his "Adagia" sound almost like corollaries. None is more telling in the context of his own art than the one which states, "The poet seems to confer his identity on the reader. It is easiest to recognize this when listening to music—I mean this sort of thing: the transference." In the context of his life, few are more revealing than these:

> The relation of art to life is of the first importance in a skeptical age since, in the absence of a belief in God, the mind turns to its own creations and examines them, not alone from the aesthetic point of view, but for what they reveal, for what they validate, for the support that they give.

> The poet is the intermediary between people and the world in which they live and also, between people as between themselves; but not between people and some other world.

He held tenaciously to the belief that poetry served "great ends"; but if the role of the poet was "to help people to live their lives" (and, even more pointedly, to help the poet to live his own life), its function was nevertheless "not to lead people out of the confusion in which they find themselves" nor "to comfort them while they follow their leaders to and fro." Its solaces were those of any other pure art; they were not, in any conventional sense, psychologically or sociologically therapeutic, nor philosophically edifying. Poetry provided an opportunity for the experience of private, individual freedom; as a "cure of the mind" and a safeguard against "the malady of the quotidian," it was "a source of pleasure and satisfaction."

His letters are full of information invaluable to anyone

interested in knowing about the man as well as about the poet and the poems, and some of the most revealing, oddly enough, are to correspondents he had never met. "Oddly enough," because he also said, "We are intimate with people we have never seen and, unhappily, they are intimate with us." But what he cherished in a correspondent was exactly the quality he demanded of a poet, of himself as a "man of imagination": evidence that the response to him and to his work (when the correspondence concerned his poetry) had come not out of curiosity about the "goings-on" of his mind merely as "goings-on," nor out of "complaisance," but as the result of a "quickening."

As his confidence in the mastery of an idiom and style of his own increased, the diffidence, brusqueness, and intolerances which puzzled a good many of his contemporaries began to disappear. The inconsistencies, contradictions, paradoxes, and ambiguities in his poetic practice and theory remained unresolved, but they in no way limited his achievement; indeed, his last poems are possessed of a radiance and warmth equalled only by their certitude. He concluded, with considerable amiability, that "poetry is the sum of its attributes." To a large degree, the same may be said of the man himself.

I. BEGINNINGS (1879–1916)

ACCORDING TO Witter Bynner, Wallace Stevens left Harvard in 1900 determined to be a poet. He had come to Cambridge from Reading, Pennsylvania, in the fall of 1897, as a special student, with literary ambitions his father had not only tolerated but encouraged; and from the point of view of his fellow undergraduates at least, he had won by the end of his junior year all the literary honors Harvard had to offer. He had been a regular contributor to the *Advocate* from the fall of his sophomore year, a member of its Literary Board from the spring of 1899, and its President from March 1900. He had published work in the *Harvard Monthly*, the *Advocate*'s rival. He had been chosen to write the "Ode" for the Junior Dinner of his class. From his own point of view, the most important—certainly the most memorable—influence on his decision to become a poet must have been his meetings with George Santayana, which he never forgot, and which he recalled to a younger friend years later:

> I doubt if Santayana was any more isolated at Cambridge than he wished to be. While I did not take any of his courses and never heard him lecture, he invited me to come to see him a number of times and, in that way, I came to know him a little. I read several poems to him and he expressed his own view of the subject of them in a sonnet which he

sent me, and which is in one of his books. This was
forty years ago, when I was a boy and when he was
not yet in mid-life. Obviously, his mind was full of
the great projects of his future and, while some of
these have been realized, it is possible to think that
many have not. It would be easy to speak of his interest and sympathy; it might amuse you more to
know that Sparklets were then something new and
that Santayana likes to toy with them as he charged
the water which he used to make a highball or two.
They seemed to excite him. I always came away
from my visits to him feeling that he made up in
the most genuine way for many things that I needed.
He was then still definitely a poet.

Yet he also recalled that as much as he had enjoyed writing
"an occasional poem for the *Advocate,*" he had not taken
poetry seriously at Harvard; he had indulged his imagination
as "part of his education," and without any intention of trying to make a career of letters.

Here his unusually good memory failed him. Or it may
have been that he never quite outgrew the uncomfortable
feeling his earliest work always seemed to give him in later
years. "Some of one's early things give one the creeps," he
told Donald Hall when thirteen of the undergraduate poems
were selected for *The Harvard Advocate Anthology* in 1951.
Moreover, he liked to say that everything he had as a poet
was his own, and that he was not conscious of owing anything to any other poet, as if his juvenilia never had existed.
Even so, the published excerpts from the journal he began to
keep in 1898 suggest that he was at least very serious about
himself, his reading, and the possibility of being "a great
poet"; they have almost nothing to say about his day-to-day
experience, his friends and acquaintances and the facts of
his life as a student. Murray Seasongood, who served on the
Advocate Board with Stevens, and later became Mayor of
Cincinnati, recalled him as

a large, handsome, healthy, robust, amiable person,
with light curly hair and the most friendly of smiles
and dispositions. To keep up with his rolling, vig-
orous gait and animated, frank and amusing talk,
while striding alongside of him was both a feat and
a privilege. He was modest, almost diffident, and
very tolerant and kindly towards, alike, his colleagues and contributors of manuscripts. Even then
a magnificent craftsman, he could write noble sonnets, odes and mighty lines in the traditional forms
of poetry.

With a solemnity characteristic of the young, however, Stevens
himself viewed his pleasant career at Harvard and his ambitions for the future somewhat less flatteringly. "I do not want
to have to make a petty struggle for existence—physical or
literary," he wrote in his journal in June 1900. "I must try
not to be a dilettante—half dream, half deed. I must be all
dream or all deed." The twenty poems and ten stories and
sketches he had published as an undergraduate already belonged to a world he assumed he was leaving behind him for
good, along with "all the surroundings" he knew: "Reading,
Berkeley, the mountains—and perhaps the clouds." Like most
of his contemporaries, he was confident that he could master
life. He took for granted his faith in being able to do what
he wanted to do; the country was still the land of opportunity for anyone willing to work hard, and material success of
some kind was not beyond his grasp. Having decided to try
the classic career of journalism in New York as an entree
into literature and, if that failed, to "knock about the country—the world" as "the only way, directed as I am more or
less strongly by the hopes and desires of my parents and
myself, of realizing to the last degree any of the ambitions
I have formed," he set off to acquire some experience of the
city.

He found New York both exhilarating and depressing. His
college connections, including a letter of introduction from
Charles Townsend Copeland, who had been his instructor in

English A and English 7, proved more or less useful, as did
his acquaintance with Harvard men a little older than he,
who had ambitions similar to his own and had already embarked on their careers. Within two weeks he had a job as a
reporter on the *Tribune*, for which he was "paid according
to the space" he could fill. He dined occasionally with Harvard friends, frequented the Harvard Club (where he read
the *Harvard Monthly*), had time to wonder whether literature
was "really a profession"—"Can you single it out, or must
you let it decide in you for itself?"—and came to the conclusion that whatever he might eventually do, he would not
"*try* to suit anybody" except himself. His high spirits failed
him now and then, but he did not take his job altogether
seriously, nor did he despair of his future: the story told by
William Carlos Williams that Stevens once contemplated
suicide because of his failure as a reporter but instead wrote
a feature story about the flotsam in the East River, "which
has since become a minor classic among newspapermen,"
seems to be apocryphal.

While "loafing" and waiting for something newsworthy
to happen, he read a good deal of poetry, especially sonnets,
and planned and wrote some, including a genteelly pathetic
lyric, "A Window in the Slums," finished a few days before
he attended the funeral of Stephen Crane. Crane "deserved
something better than [the] absolutely common-place, bare,
silly service" he got, which made Stevens realize that "there
are few hero-worshippers. . . . Therefore, few heroes." That
he should have been so deeply impressed by Crane, who, he
said, "lived a brave, aspiring, hard-working life," may seem
in retrospect almost as surprising as his admiration of "Nearer
My God to Thee," which he thought "the only appropriate
hymn for funerals"; but it adds a dimension to his youthful
figure, and makes it less remote and withdrawn than it might
otherwise be. Crane was, for many young men of Stevens's
generation who were genuinely serious about writing (or in
love with the idea of being writers) almost as romantic a
figure as Crane's own hero, Richard Harding Davis.

Stevens made a handful of new friends and acquaintances in the city, but the journal as we have it hardly mentions them. He visited the Lutheran parochial school in Brooklyn he had attended some years before, but found he could not remember the names of his schoolmates. On the whole, he enjoyed himself, found time to absorb local color and compare his liking for New York with his liking for Reading, ate well whenever he could afford it and sometimes did not eat at all, kept his sense of humor and cultivated his detachment, hoped to save enough money to go to Paris, or to Arizona or Mexico, celebrated New Year's Eve alone in his room by observing, "I still remain W. S. [and] can say *adieu!* to no part of me," made a rough draft of "Olivia: A Romantic Comedy" inspired by a performance of "Captain Jinks of the Horse Marines" in which Ethel Barrymore played Mme. Trentoni, tried to persuade his father that he should give up his job on the *Tribune* and devote all his time to writing, and, ultimately, took his father's advice and entered law school.

Except for the brief vacations he spent in Reading and a notable trip to the Canadian Rockies with W. G. Peckham, under whom he served his clerkship, Stevens concentrated all his energy on study during the next two years at New York Law School. He was awarded his law degree in June 1903, took his bar exams a year later, and, after a visit to Reading, returned to the city in September 1904, to set up practice with Lyman Ward, whom he had known "by sight" at Harvard, but had come to know better in New York. Walking along the Palisades or in northern New Jersey had provided the respite he needed from the "terrible imprisonment" of the city and what he called "terrible self-contemplation," as well as from his fear of the "years of lack of exercise" he saw stretching before him. As with Thoreau, the length and interest of his journal entries depended in large measure upon the length of his walks; and he sometimes waxed as poetic and speculative as the Concord bachelor, although in more self-indulgent and sensuously romantic terms. His fanciful and

imaginative flights, as Arcadian and Vagabondian as his
philosophic musings were youthfully sophisticated and self-
centered, showed, even so, a growing sense of his own conception of the world. He had moments of something akin to
self-pity and abnegation, although he recorded them with a
due sense of the occasion, invoking Colin Clout in his resolve
to give up "booze" and "to smoke wisely," and, with equal
literary flair, evoking his pleasure in "a flood of drinks from
crème de cassis melée, through Burgundy, Chablis etc. to
sloe gin with Mexican cigars [and] French cigaroots," when
he was able to afford them. Although he had not yet found
himself in the business world—his partnership with Ward
failed, and he more or less marked time in a number of law
firms until 1908, when he joined the New York office of the
American Bonding Company—he had completed his professional training. Law would be his career; whether he would
be the poet he still had ambition to be remained to be seen.

His "failure" as a journalist can certainly be attributed to
his temperament rather than to any real lack of ability to do
what he was asked to do and make a respectable job of it.
So far as writing was concerned, his interest was already
much more intense in his own imaginative view of things
than in people or politics and the ordinary and conventional
stuff of reporting. What he wanted to be free to explore was
"the indefinite, the impersonal, atmospheres and oceans and,
above all, the principle of order," as he came to call it, which
had a good deal in common with the way the Impressionist
painters saw the world. Nature and *plein air* were his retreat and the source of his greatest satisfaction; and if his
solitary pleasure in tinkling streams, the moon shining "from
a strange azure of its own creating," or "pine tops and the
flaring patches of snow" was almost Keatsian in its extravagance, it was nothing he had acquired at second hand, although he recorded it with greater precision and freedom in
his college sketches and his journal than in the early poems.
His accounts in the surviving letters to his mother of summers at Ephrata and Ivyland (1895–96) balance the later

journal entries; they are full of adolescent high spirits and humor, bravado and caricature:

> The piping of flamboyant flutes, the wriggling of shrieking fifes with rasping dagger-voices, the sighing of bass-viols, drums that beat and rattle, the crescendo of cracked trombones—harmonized, that is Innes band. Red geraniums, sweet-lyssoms, low, heavy quince trees, the mayor's lamps, Garrett playing on the organ, water-lilies and poultry— that is Ivyland. A shade tree, meagre grass, a peaky, waxen house, a zither, several books of poetry, a pleasant room —mine—that is our house. An antique bureau, daguerreotypes of some ancient people, a shoe case, a wash-stand, an ill-fed carpet, a featherbed reaching to my girth, with linen trappings, that is my room by day. Gloomy cadaverous shadows, a ha'moon, astride a crowing cock on a gilded weather-vane, a chair which when I attempt to sit upon it moans itself to sleep, a clock—oh that clock—it is a vigilant sentinal of the hours but its alarms are premature and unnerving, every quarter hour or so the trembling creature springs with a whirr into its covert among the depths of the springs—that is my room by night.
> A Puritan who revels in catechisms and creeds, a hand-to-mouth man, earnest, determined, discreet —Uncle Isaac. A self-sacrificing, whole-souled woman who says not much but too well—that is Aunt Mariah.
> Emma—well Emma reminds me of a tub of lillies —you must pull aside the leaves to see the flowers.

It would be easy to overstate the significance of such bits of the authentic Stevensian manner, but certainly his eye was already appreciative of the telling and eccentric detail and his ear was attuned to comic dissonances. Robert Buttel has suggested that some of the stories—"Hawkins of Cold Cape" and "In the Dead of Night"—which Stevens contributed to the *Advocate* can be characterized as "something between a college humor sketch and some of Washington Irving's burlesques

of the ghostly in *Tales of a Traveller,"* but whatever their
literary analogues may be, it is more likely that summer
holidays at Ephrata and Ivyland contributed as much to
their waywardness as the local colorists and comic writers
popular with undergraduates in the nineties.

Moreover, the world in which Stevens grew up was more
sophisticated, socially and culturally, than we may think.
Towns and small cities like Reading, or Bangor, Maine, or
Danbury, Connecticut, were certainly provincial in a great
many ways, but they were by no means so contemptible or
laughable as Mrs. Wharton or Henry James sometimes made
them out to be. Their Browning circles and choral societies,
family reunions, local pageants and church suppers and
bazaars, like the political opinions and social conscience of
their civic leaders or the importance attached to good manners, were generally conservative and a little out of date, but
they gave coherence and identity to a solidly middle-class
and successful way of life that had not yet become obsolete.
Its pretensions and prejudices were no more flagrant than
those of any other more or less self-contained community;
and they fostered as much individuality as conformity.

What this "good life" lacked in intellectual finesse and
high-mindedness it partly made up for in expansiveness. Mr.
Dooley, Horatio Alger, Frank Stockton, Bulwer-Lytton, and
James Whitcomb Riley probably provided more satisfaction
in their own way than Emerson, Carlyle, and Tennyson, or
Scott, Keats, and Jane Austen, even for families that were
"great readers." Popular culture allowed plenty of room for
individual freedom of taste, and such as it was, literary enter-
tainment or edification was freer of what Auden has called
"literary class-consciousness" than it is today in suburbia. The
Reading Stevens remembered with so much affection in the
late years of his life had more than a little in common with
the Danbury that Charles Ives lovingly recalled in much of
his music, or the small-town world made somewhat more vivid
in the Tilbury Town poems of Edwin Arlington Robinson.
However much their basic raw material may have been

modified by other influences, there was always apparent in the work of these men, as there is in the work of most other American artists of any real consequence, evidence of something local, something native and authentic and inescapably idiosyncratic. The local idiom and syntax salted with Pennsylvania Dutch may well have been more significant in shaping Stevens's "authentic and fluent speech" than his reading of Verlaine and Mallarmé, just as the local organist's wrong notes provided Ives with some of the characteristic peculiarities of his style. (Stevens once told his friend Henry Church, "Personally, I like words to sound wrong.") They never wholly outgrew their own past; and without being sentimental, it is possible to say that this sense of identity is one of the distinguishing qualities of their work.

Stevens's father, Garrett Barcalow Stevens, was born in 1848, the son of a farmer, in Feasterville, Bucks County, Pennsylvania. First a country schoolteacher, and later an attorney in Reading, "with diverse political and business interests, including a bicycle factory and a steel plant at one time," he was, according to his son's memory of him in 1954,

> quite a good egg; agreeable, active. He was of Holland Dutch descent, and his father and his grandfather had been farmers. . . . We were all great readers and the old man used to delight in retiring to the room called the library on a Sunday afternoon to read a five-or-six hundred page novel. . . . When I was younger, I always used to think that I got my practical side from my father, and my imagination from my mother. I decided to be a lawyer the same way I decided to be a Presbyterian; the same way I decided to be a Democrat. My father was a lawyer, a Presbyterian and a Democrat.

To this thumbnail sketch should be added Stevens's other comments recorded in the *Letters,* as well as the letters his father wrote to him at Harvard between 1897 and 1899, and a few other facts. Garrett Stevens was an amateur poet and

writer of sketches and stories, most of which appeared anony-
mously in the local papers, and none of which, apparently,
evoked the admiration or praise of his son. He was scrupu-
lously impartial in his treatment of all five of his children—
three sons and two daughters. He also seems to have been
somewhat distant as a father, generous and unselfish and
strongly persuaded that his sons should and could make their
own way in the world once they were provided with a sound
education. Stevens once recalled that "he wasn't a man given
to pushing his way. He needed what all of us need, and what
most of us don't get: that is to say, discreet affection." He
also said, "[H]e must have concealed . . . many things . . .
because he was one of the most uncommunicative of men.
Had he been more selfish than he was, everything would
have been different for him, so that I am bound to think
well of him."

That Stevens got more than his practical side from his
father became clear to him in later years. He, too, was in
many ways uncommunicative: he once wrote to his daughter
Holly, "My own stubbornnesses and taciturn eras are straight
out of Holland and I cannot change them any more than I
can take off my skin. But I never hesitate to seek to undo any
damage I may have done." Like his father, he felt a deep
need for a life of his own; without that privacy he could not
have been a poet. He might, indeed, have been speaking of
himself, when he said of his father, "The greater part of his
life was spent at his office; he wanted quiet, and in that quiet,
to create a life of his own."

In spite of his uncommunicativeness, Garrett Stevens was
more than a little interested in his son's literary ambitions.
He kept track of his progress at college, and from the very
beginning looked with good humor on a "liberal education"
which he once defined as learning to "feel at home among
the paintings and statuary that Bostonese vote elegant and
worthy of their admiration." And he also gave Wallace
advice:

A little romance is essential to ecstasy. We are all selfish—Self Denial doesn't seem to be a good thing excepting in others—the world holds an unoccupied niche only for those who climb up—work and study, study and work—are worth a decade of dreams— and romantic notions—but I do not believe in being so thoroughly practical that what is artistic—what is delicate or what is grand—must always be deferred to what is useful. And there is no better exercise than an effort to do our best to appreciate and de- scribe to others the beauties of those things which are denied to the vision of the absent. . . .

When we try to picture what we see, the purely imaginary is transcended, like listening in the dark we seem to really hear what we are listening for— but describing real objects one can draw straight or curved lines and the thing may be mathematically demonstrated—but who does not prefer the sunlight— and the shadow reflected.

"Paint truth but not always in drab clothes," he advised. "Catch the reflected sun-rays, get pleasurable emotions— instead of stings and tears." Again and again, those letters to which we have access indicate a common bond of tem- perament. "[T]he refinement in Sculpture," he wrote, "is not mere outline, pose, proportion [and] such—but the delicacy or courage of the artist who picks with pin point or pounds with a sledge . . ."; and in another letter, he said:

You have discovered, I suppose, that the sun is not a ball of fire sending light and heat—like a stove— but that radiation and reflection is the mystery—and that the higher up we get—and nearer to the sun the colder it gets—and a few old things like that— but are you taught and directed in your studies in a way that you must acknowledge widens your range of vision and upsets your previous notions—teaches you to think—compels you [to] reason—and provides you with the positive facts by which you know a

conclusion is correct. When this comes to you—you
will first begin to absorb and philosophize—and but
for eccentricities in your genius you may be fitted for
a Chair—Do not be contented with a smattering of
all things—be strong in something.

"All our pleasures," he confessed, "so depend upon our self
gratification—that to simply work and achieve results means
nothing—unless it [is] with a purpose in view"; and he added,

> . . . if one wanted to go to London to see some par-
> ticular thing which could not be seen save in London
> and to see which seemed indispensible to some
> achievement or purpose—he would find the means
> of getting there himself. He would cultivate the
> talent, and ability he had and sell its product for
> the means of enabling him to indulge his curiosity.
> That has been my philosophy and I soon found I
> could do it—

Both father and son could show their feelings more successfully through the written word than face to face, and in
both the struggle between the practical and the poetic was
fairly constant, however different their ideas of the poetic
may have been.

If there was a barrier between them, it was not impenetrable. Mr. Stevens wrote Wallace in February 1899, after
the appearance of "Who Lies Dead?" and "Vita Mea" in
the *Advocate*, "I am convinced from the Poetry (?) you write
your mother that the afflatus is not serious—and does not
interfere with some real hard work." But a month later,
after congratulating him on his election to the *Advocate*
Board, he wrote,

> The feeling that what one publishes is more impor-
> tant than what one thinks or writes will be with you
> to compress your likings into what your readers will
> like—and the experience will be a good one—It is all

right to talk gush and nonsense—but to see it in cold type don't seem worth while—and yet—there will be but half a column in the Advocate if you suppress all that is not brilliant and philosophical— eh!—Pleased to see a copy now and then—and to sift its grist through my unromantic sieve—

And he confessed, "You will be like I was myself at 16— bound to 'paddle your own canoe' without help from home of any substantial character." Whether Stevens remembered these remarks, or was offended by them, it is impossible to say; but forty years later in replying to a questionnaire from the *Partisan Review*, he said, "Writing poetry is one thing; publishing it is another. Often I wish that I did not publish it, because the act of publishing it invokes a seriousness different from the seriousness of writing it." Though the standards by which Stevens and his father measured literary excellence were poles apart, they also had something in common.

Stevens's mother, Margaretha Catharine Zeller, was a schoolteacher, the daughter of a shoemaker who "was far above the average from the point of view of ambition and the will to get on." She was Wallace's first confidante, to whom he could "let go" and indulge his opinions, and his "indifferent muse." "My mother just kept house and ran the family," he remembered. Except for the four letters he wrote to her in 1895–96, almost the only surviving first-hand information about his feelings toward her comes from the last two entries in his journal, written at the time of her death in 1912, a year after that of her husband. It was she, he felt, who had given life at home its stability and warmth:

I remember her studious touch at the piano, out of practice, and her absorbed, detached way of singing. At one period, say twenty years ago, she made efforts to get new things and many such objects remain: things in the parlor etc. Her way of keeping

things, of arranging rugs, of placing pieces of furni-
ture, remains unaltered. A chair is where it is because she just put it there and kept it there. The
house is a huge volume full of the story of her thirty-
five years or more within it.

Deeply as he felt about his old home in Reading and his
life there, the family was not, as one writer familiar with
his early years has said, closely knit. Everyone was free to
pursue his own interests in his own way. Stevens himself
flunked a year at high school because of "too many nights
out," and then was graduated "with merit," having won the
Alumni Medal for Oration with a piece called "The Greatest
Need of the Age," as well as the the *Reading Eagle* prize
for "The Thessalians," which he delivered at his commence-
ment. He had already outgrown, as he was to say at the age
of twenty, "those cynical years when [he] was about twelve,"
that had "subdued natural and easy flow of feelings." But
he was also writing poetry. "Autumn," which seems to have
been the first of his poems to be published, appeared in the
Reading Boys' High School magazine, *The Red and Black*,
in January 1898, during his freshman year at Harvard.

Stevens's brother and sisters took their life at home and
relations with their parents more simply. Garrett Barcalow,
Jr., who was nearly two years older than Wallace, was at
Yale for a time, but left to read law in Carlisle, and became
a lawyer in Cleveland; John Bergen, a year younger, attended
the University of Pennsylvania, entered his father's law office,
and later was named a judge in Reading. Stevens's sisters
were the youngest children. Elizabeth did social work until
her marriage in 1916; Mary Katharine, the only child still
at home at the time of Mrs. Stevens's death, died in 1919
in France, where she had been working for the Red Cross.
That she had died so far away from home horrified Stevens;
and her death, he said, ended the part of his life that he associated with his mother.

He seems not to have kept in particularly close touch

with his family after his marriage to Elsie Moll in 1909. Until the forties, he seldom visited Reading: there were too many relatives to visit, he once said, and too many calls upon his early feelings for the world in which he had grown up. When he did return, he found the city "old-fashioned" but not unpleasant. The deaths of his brothers and sisters, all of whom he outlived, shook him; and the interest in family history and genealogy, which his wife shared with him, was undoubtedly sharpened by the fact that he was the last of his generation. He was eager to join the St. Nicholas Society and the Holland Society, to prove his descent from Dutch rather than German ancestry, and he was as pleased as his wife to discover that she was of Swiss descent. Neither the Stevenses nor his wife's family belonged to Reading aristocracy—they were not, for example, members of the local Assembly—but the Stevenses were highly respected and lived in a fashionable section of the city. Elsie's family had not achieved an equal prominence; and although she was known as one of the most beautiful girls in Reading, she did not have the "advantages" important to position in a class-conscious society. She left high school during her freshman year "to go to work in a department store, where she played the piano in the sheet-music department," and "also gave piano lessons in order to help the family financially, for her parents were not wealthy." Seven years younger than her husband, she clung to her ties at home more tenaciously than he; and she seems never to have enjoyed his business or literary associates. How much his literary ambitions contributed to the "blow-ups of the nerves" between him and his wife, to which he confessed, it is impossible to say. There is little in the *Letters* to indicate much more than vast differences in taste and interests and Stevens's determination to master the dissensions they may have caused even as he pursued his own course. No confidences are violated; no deep intimacies are revealed. The sense of propriety and discretion is insistent; but the affection is clear. She felt even more strongly than he that any inquiry into the relation of his

life to his work was an unpardonable invasion of privacy—
his poetry, she said, was a relaxation from the pressures of
his business life; but she also admitted that for a long time
she had had no notion how remarkable his achievement as
a poet was nor of the high regard in which his work was
held. She became, after his death, almost a recluse; and she
never fully recovered from a stroke early in 1955, which
she suffered before his final illness.

Stevens himself was never socially ambitious in any obvious
way. "Success," he noted in the "Adagia," "is to be happy
with the wise." But he also said, "Money is a kind of poetry,"
and he openly valued it more than most other poets have
done. When asked whether he had been able to make a living
by writing, he replied:

> I have not tried to make a living by writing. How-
> ever, the fact that writers commonly take advantage
> of "such crutches as teaching and editorial work"
> is nothing that entitles writers to indulge themselves
> in spasms of self-pity. Most people avail themselves
> of crutches of one sort or another: lawyers promote
> business enterprises; doctors marry rich women and
> buy and sell securities.

Even so, everything about his forebears was "precious" to
him; and the warmth with which he evoked the mingled
memory of his own past and his feeling for the country
around Reading in some of the late poems—"The Bed of
Old John Zeller," "A Completely New Set of Objects," "Late
Hymn from the Myrrh Mountain," "The Old Lutheran Bells
at Home"—is sufficient testimony to the accuracy of his statement. It was in these late years that he came to feel that
"home is where one grows up"; more than anything else,
perhaps, this burst of sentiment deepened the tone of his
final books. That he also said of Connecticut, "I was not born
myself in the state. It is not that I am a native, but that I
feel like one," in no way lessened the depth of his feeling
for his past.

Yet he was not much given to reminiscence. He recalled walks with Edwin Livingood, the friend he saw most often as a boy and young man in Reading, who introduced him to Goethe, was a "fanatic . . . on the country wine," and was in Cambridge for graduate study during his own sophomore year: "They walked together, stopped, drank a bottle of claret together, ate cheese, walnuts, and walking back home, [Livingood] recited poetry—going through the woods—very loud. Very clear." Other friends recalled expeditions to Mount Penn, at the top of which stood the Chinese pagoda advertising confectionery, which was to suggest the setting for "Three Travelers Watch a Sunrise," and to Kuechler's Roost, an inn where the chicken wings and radishes were famous. Stevens was the witty member of the group, according to one old friend, the young sophisticate who sometimes brought interesting visitors home from New York to spend holidays and vacations with him. But he frequently spent his time alone. One early journal entry records in details that Hawthorne would have admired his enjoyment of a solitary winter walk over the mountain, and then adds,

> I forget what I was thinking of—except that I wondered why people took books into the woods to read in summertime when there was so much to read there that one could not find in books. . . . Coming home I saw the sun go down behind a veil of grime. It was rather terrifying I confess from an allegorical point of view. But that is usually the case with allegory.

During his long courtship of Elsie, whom he first met during a holiday from his studies, he was often in Reading, but the surviving excerpts from his letters to her are mostly concerned with the private and idealized world he envisioned for them together. Seldom did the quotidian present intrude itself upon that vision. "I lost a world," he once wrote to her, "when I left Reading"; and one other notable letter, written a few months before their marriage, is full of delighted

memories of his "bicycle days." Both the halcyon world he
conjured up as theirs and the one that he recalled had a
vividness far surpassing the more delicate one suggested in
the lyrics he sent her in "The Little June Book" and its companion on her birthdays. He was sure that Reading lay behind him; and it was not until almost thirty years later that
his "world of small beginnings," as seen in an old city di-
rectory—"a kind of Book of Grandfathers"—sent to him by a
relative, touched him so deeply again.

Except for the earliest years, the period between 1910 and
1915 is the most sparsely documented. Most of his energy
after his marriage went into his career in business, although
his letters to Elsie during the summers she spent in Reading
or Vinemont, or at Pocono Manor, reveal his unflagging interest in "poetizing." Elsie still hoped, in 1911, for a home in
Reading; but if he returned, he said, "I should want to go
into a business—and that requires capital and experience and a
willingness to make money 1¾ cents at a time." He was determined to make his career in insurance and law; his ad-
vancements were already giving him a living and offered
possibilities. If by "hard and faithful work" he succeeded,
he might find time and the means to indulge his passion for
poetry, which meant, he had already begun to realize, no
more to her than "the things to be done in a place like New
York," but which had nearly everything to do with his own
life: visits to the Metropolitan Museum of Art; "the wise sayings of K'Ung Fu-Tzu . . . and the poetry of the Wanamaker
advertisements"; Delacroix; a phrase ("j'ai le gout de l'azur")
he had found in the poems of the Comtesse de Noailles, which
he had dropped in to the New York Public Library to read;
Chinese and Japanese jades and porcelains at the American
Art Galleries—"Cucumber-green, camellia-leaf-green, apple-
green etc. moonlight, blue, etc. ox-blood, chicken-blood, cherry,
peach-blow etc. etc. Oh! and mirror-black: that is so black
and with such a glaze that you can see yourself in it"; the
occasional companionship of literary and business friends, and
the expansiveness of cigars and good food and drink (although

he told his sister Elizabeth that Elsie was "a stunning cook"); and even the walks he found time for in his old haunts up the Hudson and in New Jersey. He wrote her in his familiar high-spirited style, his protestations of loneliness and his wishes that she enjoy her summer and be happy juxtaposed with his excitement about those ideas and things that most interested him; and one summer he bought her a piano "because it would be a good thing for us both in the winter evenings."

Her summers made the winters in New York bearable, if never to her real liking. Adolph Alexandér Weinman, the sculptor, and their landlord at 441 West Twenty-first Street, persuaded Elsie to pose for him. The bust he made of her became the basis of his winning design for the "Liberty Head" dime and half-dollar issued in 1916. Stevens continued to prove himself to his business associates. In 1916, he became a director of the Hartford Live Stock Insurance Company, a newly formed subsidiary of the Hartford Accident and Indemnity Company, which he had joined earlier the same year, and for which he did much of his work. He was well on his way to becoming, as the *Hartford Agent* said of him in its tribute after his death, "an outstanding attorney in the bond claim field." And he was beginning to make his mark as a poet. In May, he and Elsie moved to Hartford, which was to be their home thereafter.

JUVENILIA

A HANDFUL of the stories, sketches, and poems which Stevens contributed to the *Advocate* between 1898 and 1900 showed promise if little distinction. The typical undergraduate story of that period was a heavy-handed, imperfectly plotted melodrama, an anecdotal essay in fine writing, or a proper comedy of manners involving self-consciously clever young men from one side of the Charles and the wittier, invariably charming girls who lived on the other side in Back Bay. The melodramas owed a good deal not only to Kipling and Jack London, but also to writers as various as F. Marion Crawford, Stevenson, and Hawthorne. The more sophisticated comedies paid tribute to Howells as frequently as to Wilde; for the simpler comic turns, Frank Stockton and Peter Finley Dunne provided models. Hardy and de Maupassant, perhaps, contributed a veneer of irony to a few more "serious" pieces about the moral degradation which went hand in hand with poverty or ill-advised social ambition; but not a single piece of this or any other sort called into question the political, economic, or cultural values upon which the white man's burden and a laissez-faire society rested. For most of Stevens's contemporaries interested in things literary, gentility was all.

There were exceptions. One or two were enthusiastic admirers of James Gibbons Huneker and the *vie de bohème;* for a few others, Walter Pater or Charles Eliot Norton represented the ideal for the aspiring litterateur. It was from Norton that the belief that "all the poetry had been written and all the paintings painted" had been borrowed, which was, according to Stevens himself, one of the commonplaces of the day. But whether the young aesthetes accepted the canons of taste upheld by Norton, or identified themselves with the avant garde, they were very much a minority. Those who wrote "fine prose" were more likely to be imitating Kenneth Grahame or Mary Johnston than Edgar Saltus; and although Henri de Regnier's lectures on the Symbolist poets in the spring of 1900 evoked a graceful advance endorsement and a translation of "L'Ile" from the *Advocate,* more influential poets were Tennyson, Swinburne, and the Pre-Raphaelites. But the great example for those who toyed with the idea of pursuing a literary career, whether they followed the genteel or the aesthetic tradition, was Richard Harding Davis, the epitome of success, manliness, and romance.

A few of Stevens's friends and associates did go on to make names for themselves. Pitts Sanborn, who was something of a virtuoso, and could compose a creditable sonnet on "The Girlhood of Beatrice" or handle a conventional comedy of manners with enough restraint to make it momentarily amusing, became a music critic of considerable distinction and the program annotator for the New York Philharmonic. Witter Bynner turned his student interest in the exotic to excellent account in his translations of classical Chinese poetry and his own poems of the Indian Southwest. John Macy proved to be a pioneering critic of American literature. Walter Conrad Arensberg, "who knew all there was to know about Pater," was an early translator of Mallarmé, produced some uncompromising experiments in verse for Alfred Kreymborg's *Others* (which he also helped to finance), and championed Cubism and modern art. Hughes Mearns became an educator and critic. Robert Frost, however, did not stay at Harvard long enough to make any sort of undergraduate reputation, and he and Stevens did not meet until 1935.

The stories and sketches Stevens contributed to the *Advo-*

cate only partly adhered to the formulas followed by his fellow undergraduates. He flirted with melodrama in "Her First Escapade," the plot of which involved an unfeeling rich farmer momentarily roused to jealousy when his housekeeper attempts to escape the drabness of her life by fleeing with a poor young neighbor. The farmer, firing a gun in the direction they have gone, and intending only to frighten them, accidentally and unknowingly kills the girl. Although the prose is not so much clumsy or overwrought as it is toneless, the landscape is well observed.

He was more comfortable, however, in his comic stories. "In the Dead of Night" is an extravaganza set in a house very much like his uncle's at Ivyland. Cavanaugh, a disgruntled servant dismissed for prying, takes revenge on his employers by drugging the apple dumplings served at dinner the night before he is to depart; and the effects are both astonishing and unpredictable. One visiting aunt, Mrs. Fann, is found pacing the hall shortly after midnight, wringing her hands and crying, "Oh . . . will no one fold a poor lampshade? Fold me—fold me—and put me away?"; the other, "waving an umbrella and mumbling 'Jingle Bells' to herself," goes tobogganing in a portable tub "full tilt" down the stairs and into the narrator's father "in a pair of gaudy pajamas and still more gaudy blouse," who is "haranguing" Cavanaugh "on the Philippine question." The narrator's sister appears from her room "in a walking cape and bonnet," and opening her parasol, asks, "How far is it, Tom . . . from—how far from—far from—how far is it—now Tom do tell me." From the memory of this fictitious night, "Disillusionment of Ten O'Clock" was clearly descended.

"Hawkins of Cold Cape" is a less original tale of a disenchanted newspaper editor who capitalizes on the credulity of his readers in order to take over the business wealth of the town. Using his one-legged assistant's account of a locally observed meteor as his inspiration, he invents a story based on "reports" from "metropolitan journals" that the end of the world is to take place "six days hence." To "relieve" the town's frantic citizens, Hawkins sends his assistant to buy up cows, chickens, and "anything purchasable." When the fateful night has passed and the people stream back from the shore where they have been awaiting their doom, they are greeted by two announcements on the print shop door. One states that the reports of the end of the world "were a newspaper fake"; the other, that the *Traveller* has discontinued publication, but that Hawkins "is now in a position to supply Cold Cape and vicinity with milk, cream, butter and eggs . . . at the lowest prices."

"The Nymph" is more ambitious. As a satire on a solitary self-conscious nature lover in pursuit of an Eden in which blackberries are "mures de ronce" to be shared with a nymph dressed "in a rather faded blue skirt, with a white sweater, and a spray of eglantine in her light, touselled hair," it prefigures the adventures of his later eccentrics, Carlos and Crispin. The nymph, who sees through the very aesthetic narrator, says, "I live here all alone—all alone in the woods—except for an occasional pedestrian." Her name, somewhat to the young man's dismay, turns out to be Dora; he hears it in the call of some "giant" of the woods. As he pursues her, calling after her, and hearing the echoes around him, he comes to an open space:

I stopped in bewilderment. Three large tents were spread out on the grass. In front of the tents were two black kettles hanging over fires that gave a great deal of smoke. At some distance from these kettles, at the end of the opening, were two posts connected by a rope on which a dozen or more towels were hanging in the sun. Then there was a spring wagon loaded with boxes, a table covered with newly washed pots and pans, several young men with pipes in their mouths, playing cards under a tree, and above all, fastened to a flag pole over the middle and largest tent was a banner on which I could read "The Eureka Camping Club of Billville, Mass."

Like the eggshells left by picnickers, which "desecrated" the
private temples he found on his solitary walks along the Hudson, this encounter brought Stevens face-to-face with "another
American vulgarity," as he called it in "Celle Qui Fût
Héaulmiette" fifty years later.

One other comedy, "Part of His Education," derives its
limited effectiveness from a different sort of detached and
amused self-scrutiny. Billy, who is "a regular fellow," and
Geoffrey, a fastidious aesthete, visit a barroom in order to
see "the side of life" that some of Geoffrey's fellow collegians
talk so knowingly about but which he has never seen. He
orders crème de menthe, makes an ass of himself by calling
the regular customers pigs because of their failure to appreciate a ballade, and eventually atones for his stupidity by
ordering beers all around. The happy ending hardly works,
and Billy's description of those who frequent the barroom as
"thirsty flowers longing for dew" in search of some beauty
in their lives, is as inept as Geoffrey's need to drink "the
beer of reality." How much "Part of His Education" owed
to a similar scene in *McTeague* is impossible to say; but Robert
Buttel's cogent suggestion is worth note. Without stretching
the point, it seems likely that the interest in the disparity
between "things as they are" and "things as they appear,"
which all four of these comic pieces have in common, and
which characterizes so much of his later work, was congenial
from the beginning.

Stevens had already left for New York by the time "Four
Characters," his final contribution to the *Advocate*, appeared
in print. Two of these prose sketches are as slight as anything he had published earlier. The other two looked a long
way ahead. One is a monologue which is an attempt at a
characterization of a genteel lady fallen on hard times and
reduced to running a boardinghouse; and for all its conven-
tionality, it is full of touches as authentic as anything he had
yet achieved. It was suggested, one may assume, by his own
experience at 54 Garden Street, where he lived in a rooming
house run by the daughters of Theophilus Parsons, who had

once been Dane Professor of Law at Harvard. Like so many other memories of his student days, this one underwent many metamorphoses; but the original experience meant a good deal to him, and he never forgot it. Garrett Stevens wrote to his son in the fall of 1897:

> I am much pleased to know that in living with the Misses Parsons you make them feel that it is not the mere accommodation that you admire but that their personal worth is attractive, and whatever the world may have in store for you their friendship is cherished—It is a great thing my boy—they could treat you as a mere lodger. They *could* be formal and disagreeable—and that they *have tried* to make you feel happier and better content is a compliment to you, for they are unselfish when they even say "Good Morning" and I know you would miss it if they suddenly grew indifferent.

The letter which occasioned these remarks has not survived; but by the time Stevens came to record his experience three years later, his attitude had undergone a change:

> ". . . You may have noticed when you came in that the doorway and vestibule are copies of the Temple of the Winds,—a weakness of my father's. Poor dad! He had this very room"—it was a room in the attic: the wordwork was painted brown; the wallpaper was a faded green, stained with gray where the rain had leaked through the half-ruined roof—"he had this very room painted in imitation of the Ducal Palace in Venice. I have never been to Venice; father died the summer I meant to go. But some of my friends say the imitation is quite remarkable, although I don't care much. And the garden!—the garden! How we used to dance there in the summer evenings!—with the trees bright with little lanterns, and the rose-bushes tied up with ribbons, and the sweetest orchestra of guitars and mandolins hidden somewhere in

the foliage. . . . And downstairs there was a dining-
room, with a high white ceiling and a golden chan-
delier. Well, you will see it if you decide to come.
You will see your fellow-boarders, too. There will be
a seamstress and an artist, and Smith, and an elec-
trician. But you will see, you will see!"

Further abstracted and refined by the passage of time, and
metamorphosed by his imagination, this sketch became, almost without question, "The Ordinary Women":

> Then from their poverty they rose,
> From dry catarrhs, and to guitars
> They flitted
> Through the palace walls.
>
> They flung monotony behind,
> Turned from their want, and, nonchalant,
> They crowded
> The nocturnal halls.
>
> The lacquered loges huddled there
> Mumbled zay-zay and a-zay, a-zay.
> The moonlight
> Fubbed the girandoles. . . .

The other sketch attempted a plain style, bare of orna-
ment, and intended to be suitable to its subject:

> One night I met a friend of mine who was a re-
> porter for a newspaper. He was looking up a death.
> I went with him. We climbed up the filthy stairs
> of a tenement house and knocked at the door of a
> room on the third floor. A woman of about seventy
> or seventy-five years of age answered the knock.
> She stood back and closed the door after us as we
> entered.
> "I am a reporter for the *Times,*" said my friend.

"I believe a man named Bigsby died here tonight. Can you give me any information?"

The old woman nodded, and with short little steps walked to the stove, which stood against a wall of the room. She pushed a kettle of boiling, steaming water to the back part of the stove, then returned to the table where we were standing, bent down and looked up under the shade of a feeble lamp, shaking it to get more light.

"Yes, he died here to-night. That's him."

She picked up the lamp and walked across the room to a dark corner. Two chairs had been connected with an ironing board, and on this board lay the body of an old man covered with a bed-cloth.

"That's my husband," continued the woman, pulling the cloth away from his face. "He's eighty years old, and that's pretty old, isn't it? We've always been here in this room. I took in washing, and Bigsby would sit around and smoke his pipe. No, I don't think he had any relatives—except myself."

She pulled the cloth back over the thin, shrunken features, put the lamp on the table, and went over to the stove again.

"Won't you have some tea?" she asked. "I'm just going to make some. Bigsby hated it."

We thanked her and started to go.

"I will light you to the stairs," she said. As she crossed the room the lamp lit up the hovel, and we saw a bed that had not been visible before. It was made of a tattered mattress with straw sticking out at the edges. It was perfectly bare, without pillow or sheet.

From this anecdote came a companion piece to "The Ordinary Women," published with it in the *Dial* in July 1922: "The Emperor of Ice-Cream." Stevens once said that he did not recall the circumstances under which the poem was written, "unless this means the state of mind from which it came. I dislike niggling, and like letting myself go. This poem is

an instance of letting myself go." His comment that it "wears
a deliberately commonplace costume, and yet seems . . . to
contain something of the essential gaudiness of poetry," has
provoked almost as much controversy as the poem itself; but
whatever its metaphysical and aesthetic implications may be,
it is of some consequence to know that not everything in
the Stevens canon derives from the unimpeachably correct
and acceptable sources—Laforgue, Mallarmé, Valéry—that
some of his critics have proposed. Moreover, although "The
Emperor of Ice-Cream" is a single example, it adds weight
to his statement to Ronald Lane Latimer:

> While, of course, my imagination is a most impor-
> tant factor, nevertheless I wonder whether, if you
> were to suggest any particular poem, I could not find
> an actual background for you. I have been going to
> Florida for twenty years, and all of the Florida
> poems have actual backgrounds. The real world seen
> by an imaginative man may very well seem like an
> imaginative construct.

If the original sketch published in the *Advocate* was pure
invention, it was one that stayed with him; and it confirms
—as do "Cortège for Rosenbloom," "The Shape of the Coroner," "Sunday Morning," and certain stanzas of "Le Monocle
de Mon Oncle"—his statement to Harriet Monroe that he
was "absorbed" by the subject of death.

Of his undergraduate poems, nine were Italian sonnets,
full of echoes of Keats, *The House of Life,* and Meredith, as
well as of Tennyson and the *Rubaiyat*. The division between
the octave and the sestet is carefully observed; and as exercises in organization and structure, they gave Stevens an
opportunity to work at the problem of making his bread and
butter come out even, as Frost has put it. Diction posed a
more serious problem: the tone is never sustained or secure.
His engagement with the sonnet was a purely formal one;
and it apparently never occurred to him (or to most of his
contemporaries) to try his hand at Shakespearean sonnets—

perhaps because they seemed "easier" and not very impressive tests of one's virtuosity. Unlike Robinson, who was already bending the form to his own dramatic purposes, or Trumbull Stickney, who was making some experiments influenced by Gautier and the Parnassians, he abandoned the fourteener early. He did not go so far as William Carlos Williams, who argued later that the trouble with sonnets is that "they all say the same thing"; what seems more likely is that both "Sunday Morning" and "Le Monocle de Mon Oncle" represent his imaginative transmutation of the form.

"Vita Mea" was his second contribution to the *Advocate,* and his least impressive:

With fear I trembled in the House of Life,
Hast'ning from door to door, from room to room,
Seeking a way from that impenetrable gloom
Against whose walls my strength lay weak from strife,
All dark! All dark! And what sweet wind was rife
With earth, or sea, or star, or new sun's bloom,
Lay sick and dead within that place of doom,
Where I went raving like the winter's wife.

"In vain, in vain," with bitter lips I cried;
"In vain, in vain," along the hallways died
And sank in silences away. Oppressed
I wept. Lo! through those tears the window-bars
Shone bright, where Faith and Hope like long-sought stars
First gleamed upon that prison of unrest.

If he learned in his later sonnets to count his syllables and feet, and to avoid the worst excesses of crying aloud in someone else's voice, he never found a subject of his own, or anything like a manner of his own. Even the sonnet he took to Santayana as an act of homage, suffered from strain:

Cathedrals are not built along the sea;
The tender bells would jangle on the hoar

And iron winds; the graceful turrets roar
With bitter storms the night long angrily;
And through the precious organ pipes would be
A low and constant murmur of the shore
That down those golden shafts would rudely pour
A mighty and a lasting melody.

And those who knelt within the gilded stalls
Would have vast outlook for their weary eyes.
There they would see high shadows on the walls
From passing vessels in their fall and rise;
Through gaudy windows there would come too soon
The low and splendid rising of the moon.

It is not difficult to see what interested Santayana in this effort, quite aside from its youthful paganism. In his *Interpretations of Poetry and Religion,* published a few months before the sonnet appeared in the *Harvard Monthly,* Santayana had said,

> . . . religion and poetry are identical in essence, and differ merely in the way in which they are attached to practical affairs. Poetry is called religion when it intervenes in life; and religion when it merely supervenes upon life is seen to be nothing but poetry.

The anonymous *Advocate* reviewer of *Poetry and Religion*—Stevens himself, it may have been, since as editor of the magazine he often had to furnish much of the material himself—commented at some length on this passage, and observed that

> both religion and poetry appeal to the imagination rather than to the understanding. Their function is not to discover and describe new facts of experience, but rather to remould and interpret data already given by science and reflection, in accordance with the demands of the desires and activities of our hu-

man nature. Their province is not in the realm of
scientific "reality"; it is rather in the world of values
and appreciations,—in short, of ideals. Poetry presents to us that world as an object of contempla-
tion, satisfying the demands of our nature, and yet
conceived as without practical import,—as merely
"supervening" upon our life. . . .
    Whether or not the Ideal exists as a matter of fact
is utterly irrelevant. That it exists as a matter of value
is enough for the religious consciousness. The individual ideal self for instance by which we all measure our ideals, may or may not be conceived by us,
so far as its practical value is concerned, as embodied
in some Divine self; its mere existence as a concept
of our thought is sufficient to make it a valid criterion
and end of moral action. In like manner, God may
or may not exist as an independent absolute *thing*,
an object, so to speak, for scientific exploration. He
assuredly exists as a necessary postulate of the poetic
imagination, embodying in concrete form the perfected projection of life, which alone can satisfy
the will.

All other questions aside, Santayana's thesis must have seemed
to Stevens the embodiment of the poetic doctrine he was
looking for. The problem of God—of religious feelings and
convictions—would occupy him off and on in his journal and
in his letters to Elsie, for some time to come; and although
he insisted that he was "not in the least religious," it was
not until he had written "Sunday Morning" that his own
resolution of the conflict between poetry and religion was
actually achieved. (He told one correspondent that the poem
"is not essentially a woman's meditation on religion and the
meaning of life. It is anybody's meditation. . . . The poem
is simply an expression of paganism, although, of course, I
did not think that I was expressing paganism when I wrote
it.") But as a prefiguration of "the supreme fiction" which
makes "life complete in itself," "the perfected projection of

life, which alone can satisfy the will" could hardly be more
precise. It is impossible to overlook the importance to Stevens
of Santayana's interest in him, an interest which William
Carlos Williams regretted that he never forgot, since it interfered with Stevens's own poetic character. That Santayana
remained for him a "superb figure" his own allusions in his
letters make clear; and although he told Henry Church that
in Santayana "the religious and the philosophic [were] too
dominant," "a man like Dr. Santayana" illustrated the character of the holder of the Chair of Poetry he was interested
in seeing established in order to make "the theory of poetry"
one of the significant humanities. The argument of the "Memorandum" he prepared for Church in 1942 descended as directly as the idea of "the supreme fiction" from *Poetry and
Religion:*

> The major poetic idea in the world is and always
> has been the idea of God. One of the visible move-
> ments of the modern imagination is the movement
> away from the idea of God. The poetry that created
> the idea of God will either adapt it to our different
> intelligence, or create a substitute for it, or make it
> unnecessary. These alternatives probably mean the
> same thing, but the intention is not to foster a cult.
> The knowledge of poetry is a part of philosophy, and
> a part of science; the import of poetry is the import
> of the spirit. The figures of the essential poets should
> be spiritual figures. The comedy of life or the tragedy
> of life as the material of an art, and the mold of life
> as the object of its creation are contemplated.

Nothing came of the idea; and of the "ardent" and "excited
ambitions" Stevens himself had for the project, *The Necessary Angel,* he said, was, "alas! the only realization possible."
Appropriately enough, Stevens's last act of homage to Santayana was "To an Old Philosopher in Rome," written in
the summer of 1952, not long before Santayana's death. Like
so many of the late poems, "To an Old Philosopher in Rome"

has a radiance and human warmth that illuminate his "theory"; and just as his "theory" may have derived from *Poetry and Religion*, so the humanity of "To an Old Philosopher in Rome" may owe something to a sentence in one of Santayana's letters to José Rodríguez Feo, which Stevens not only "loved" but repeated, and which might well have served as an epigraph for the poem: "I have always, somewhat sadly, bowed to expediency or fate."

But whatever Stevens learned from Santayana about "the theory of poetry" as "the theory of life," he could not learn much about the language of poetry. Santayana's sonnet in reply to "Cathedrals are not built along the sea" was composed with skill, but without the mastery of the conventions that distinguished his best work; it remained an occasional period piece about nature as God:

> For aeons had the self-responsive tide
> Risen to ebb, and tempests blown to clear,
> And the belated moon refilled her sphere
> To wane anew—for, aeons since, she died—
> When to the deeps that called her earth replied
> (Lest year should cancel unavailing year)
> And took from her dead heart the stones to rear
> A cross-shaped temple to the Crucified.
> Then the wild winds through organ-pipes descended
> To utter what they meant eternally,
> And not in vain the moon devoutly mended
> Her wasted taper, lighting Calvary,
> While with a psalmody of angels blended
> The sullen diapason of the sea.

In Stevens's quatrains and short lyrics that served as footnotes to his sonnets, the diction was easier and somewhat less strained. But it was in six poems published during the spring of 1900 that he really began to find a theme and a point of view, despite the fact that he had not discovered a form of his own. The subject matter as such was derivative, but the attitude toward it looked forward to the poet of *Harmonium.* "Ballade of the Pink Parasol" and "Outside the Hospital" owed a great deal to Austin Dobson, William Ernest Henley, and H. C. Bunner; the four "Street Songs," to Bliss Carman, the seventeenth-century song writers, and Verlaine. Even the sonnet which formed the second "Street Song" achieved a freedom he had not managed before; and the descriptive, almost imagistic lyrics with which the series opened and closed showed an élan and sprightliness quite different from the unconvincing, forced high spirits of two or three of the sonnets.

The irony of "Outside the Hospital" was neither subtle nor very penetrating, but it was sustained and all of a piece. The jaunty rhythm of the six-line stanza heightens rather than detracts from the total effect; and the concluding dialogue is dramatically well-placed:

> See the blind and lame at play,
>   There on the summer lawn—
> She with her graceless eyes of clay,
>   Quick as a frightened fawn,
> Running and tripping into his way
>   Whose legs are gone.
>
> How shall she 'scape him, where shall she fly,
>   She who never sees?
> Now he is near her, now she is by—
>   Into his arms she flees.
> Hear her gay laughter, hear her light cry
>   Among the trees.
>
> "Princess, my captive." "Master, my king."
>   "Here is a garland bright."
> "Red roses, I wonder, red with the Spring,
>   Red with a reddish light?"
> "Red roses, my princess, I ran to bring,
>   And be your knight."

More than any of the other undergraduate poems, "Outside the Hospital" illustrates an interest in "manner" rather than "matter"; and none illustrates it more successfully.

"Ballade of the Pink Parasol" also looked forward to poems in which manner was more important than matter: "Peter Parasol," "Exposition of the Contents of a Cab," "The Weeping Burgher." But however great a debt the "Ballade" owed to Dobson, Henley, or Andrew Lang, it came close to succeeding as pastiche.

> I pray thee where is the old-time wig,
>   And where is the lofty hat?
> Where is the maid on the road in her gig,
>   And where is the fire-side cat?
>   Never was sight more fair than that,
> Outshining, outreaching them all,
>   There in the night where the lovers sat—
> But where is the pink parasol?
>
> Where in the pack is the dark spadille
>   With scent of lavender sweet,
> That never was held in the mad quadrille.
>   And where are the slippered feet.
>   Ah! we'd have given a pound to meet
> The card that wrought our fall,
>   The card that none other of all could beat—
> But where is the pink parasol?
>
> Where is the roll of the old calash,
>   And the jog of the light sedan?
> Whence Chloe's diamond brooch would flash
>   And conquer poor peeping man.
>   Answer me, where is the painted fan
> And the candles bright on the wall;
>   Where is the coat of yellow and tan—
> But where is the pink parasol?

Prince, these baubles are far away,
   In the ruin of palace and hall,
Made dark by the shadow of yesterday—
But where is the pink parasol?

The "Ode" he wrote for his Junior Class Dinner a little
more than a month before he left Cambridge was a farewell
in the most appropriate Vagabondian manner:

A golden time and golden-shining hour
From out the cloudless weather
Is such an hour and time as this
That finds us here together
In May! in May!
And we are careless of the night;
We shall be ready for the day;
We shall set sail for near or far,
With a shout into the light,
And a hail to the morning star.

He had completed the first stage of his apprenticeship; and
if it had not been arduous or had produced nothing so characteristic of the mature poetry as the early poems of Frost,
Robinson, or even Eliot are of theirs, he had learned something of value. The boundaries of what was to become his
life as a poet may not have been fixed, but in retrospect, at
least, one can say that they had been glimpsed. The poems
he had written so far were such poems as Crispin must have
composed before his departure for America, when he was

. . . lutanist of fleas, the knave, the thane,
The ribboned stick, the bellowing breeches, cloak
Of China, cap of Spain, imperative haw
Of hum, inquisitorial botanist,
And general lexicographer of mute
And maidenly greenhorns . . .

The poems to come—which would not give him "the creeps"
—were fifteen years in the future.

The writing of poetry intruded itself into his experience of
the city, but it had to compete with other interests. He still
had "ideas" and "thoughts" for sonnets; but he also noted
in his journal, "Perish all sonnets! . . . Sonnets have their
place, without mentioning names; but they can also be found
tremendously out of place: in real life where things are quick,
unaccountable, responsive." "Real life" meant not only the
world in which one made a living, important as that world
was and would remain (sometimes to the point of making
him appear to discount the value of writing, at least as some
of his critics have read "The Comedian as the Letter C" and
other ironic poems). "Real life" meant also the excitement of
new experience, the pleasure of "being" a poet, of "merely
circulating," which even Santayana thought was as important
as "writing poetry," although not in the sense in which either
the Decadent poets or those who preached the cult of experience according to Samuel Butler meant the phrase; and
it was a pleasure he never outgrew: "The collecting of poetry
from one's experience as one goes along," he said in the
"Adagia," "is not the same thing as merely writing poetry."

The difficulty lay in learning how to distinguish the one
from the other and in discovering how to do justice to both.
As "the sound of life or the color of life," poetry was something he could not find in Stedman's *Victorian Anthology* or
the sonnets of David Gray (which almost brought tears to his
eyes, but which, for all their beauty, lacked "any great degree
of force—other than pathetic"). It was also more than walking
down West Street, along the North River, "the most interesting street in the city," more than the weather, or the "crown"
of imagination he wore and the "air" he was sometimes all
too conscious of walking on—that world of his own which was
frequently at odds with "real life." He was not so self-indulgent
as to find the *vie de bohème* particularly attractive; nor did it
occur to him to think that he would not have to make his
own way in the "real" world. He never considered being a

teacher; business or law would provide a more plausible alternative to journalism. In spite of his desire to go to Paris, he would not go unless he had a good reason, which for him meant a practical reason. "I could enjoy mornings in Florida and afternoons and long nights in California . . . away from the endless chain to which I am fastened like a link," he said. "But Florida and California are limited regions [and] my desire is limited." In due course, he would have his mornings (and afternoons and nights—"breathing fresh air and living at leisure") in Florida, although not, to begin with, by way of vacation but as a consequence of his claims work; and he would also have, and come to prefer to Paris itself, an imagined city created by correspondence with his bookseller who bought him French paintings and sent him French books, who helped to create that "poetic atmosphere" in which he could live, like Crispin, "a life without the slightest adventure." Other correspondents would do the same for him: Leonard Van Geyzel in Ceylon, Thomas McGreevy in Dublin; in the meantime, other friends would bring him his annual bonbons from Europe.

And although poetry was always an "escape," it was also "a response to the daily necessity of getting the world right," just as "a poem should stimulate some sense of being and of being alive." Mastery of the sonnet or the ballade paled beside learning to make the most of the commonplace. In one of his less enthusiastic moments during his first days in New York, he wrote,

> I can hardly believe that Wily's garden [in Berkeley, Pennsylvania] . . . is as fine a thing as it was last summer. I am going up there, however, some day [and] shall see for myself. I miss my diary of last year, which is still in Cambridge. If it was here I could live over a few days at least. Now my flowers are all in milliner's windows [and] in tin-cans on fifth-story fire-escapes.

Determined as he was to live life in a poetic atmosphere,

only part of which he could create by his own efforts, he could not escape the quotidian. There was a poetry of flowers in milliners' windows and in tin cans on fire escapes as well as the poetry of Wily's garden. If, like the Canon in "Notes toward a Supreme Fiction," he "had to choose," he already sensed that

> . . . it was not a choice
> Between excluding things. It was not a choice
>
> Between, but of.

But to make the most of the commonplace would also mean being able to achieve a perspective on Wily's garden and flowers in tin cans which would include them both: the perspective of a "connoisseur of chaos" or of "the man on the dump," an affluence of well-being and material success as well as of imagination, the one supporting and informing the other. The choice was never, of course, either-or; and although it is, perhaps, only in retrospect that it seems to have been "of," or to have been a conscious choice at all, it seems clear that within the limitations of his own desires,

> He chose to include the things
> That in each other are included, the whole,
> The complicate, the amassing harmony.

II. 1914–1930

Harriet Monroe's claim that *Poetry* "discovered" Stevens cannot be disputed, despite the appearance of eight poems in the *Trend* for September 1914, two months before the publication of "Phases" in *Poetry's* "War Number." Pitts Sanborn, who had joined the staff of the *Trend* earlier that year and had helped give its genteel pages something of a genteelly avant-garde look, was undoubtedly responsible for obtaining the lyrics to which Stevens gave the collective title "Carnet de Voyage," as well as the two short poems published in the November issue shortly after Carl Van Vechten had taken over the editorship. For five poems of the "Carnet de Voyage" group, Stevens rifled "The Little June Book" he had put together for Elsie in 1909; but there is little in any of the five other poems printed in the *Trend* to suggest that they might have been written later. Indeed, one of the pieces in the November issue had been salvaged from the "June Book" of 1908.

Stevens had not intended to publish these exercises in poetic textures, at least when he wrote them; but he had not forgotten them, and Sanborn may have seen some of them on one or another of the occasions when he and Stevens met Walter Arensberg, Witter Bynner, and other Harvard friends to talk about the arts and the literary life. To Sanborn, perhaps, goes the credit for having persuaded Stevens to publish at all; but a poet who was as eager as Stevens had been in

1904–05 "to make a music of [his] own, a literature of [his] own," and "to live [his] own life"—"To live in the world but outside of existing conceptions of it," as he later put it— would eventually have sought publication. Looking back from the vantage point of his seventy-fifth year and his *Collected Poems*, he could say that he had been no more serious about poetry during his early days in New York than he had been at Harvard; and that he had nothing more substantial to offer Sanborn than the poems of the "June Books" suggests that he had written little in five years or that his poetic ambitions had flagged. The published excerpts from his journal and his letters to Elsie, however, indicate that the opposite was true, at least up to the time of their marriage in 1909; and the few surviving letters written between 1910 and 1913 reveal how persistent his interest was. In 1913, he wrote to her,

> I have . . . been trying to get together a little collec-
> tion of verses again; and although they are simple to
> read, when they're done, it's a deuce of a job (for
> me) to do them. Keep all this a great secret. There
> is something absurd about all this writing of verses;
> but the truth is, it elates and satisfies me to do it. It
> is an all-round exercise quite superior to ordinary
> reading. So that, you see, my habits are positively
> lady-like.

Such secrecy seems hardly appropriate to the fanciful, insubstantial lyrics he once called "Intermezzi," and their immaturity and lack of any clearly defined poetic character may already have been embarrassing to him at the age of thirty-three. In their echoes of Bliss Carman, Verlaine's *Fêtes Galantes*, or Judith Gautier's *Le Livre de Jade*, as well as of Stevenson, Keats, and the glimmering midnights of the early Yeats, they were more self-indulgent and in some ways even less accomplished than the poems he had written at Harvard. The handful of more recent pieces showed more sophistication; and in the lively and uncritical artistic ferment of 1914, the synaesthesia of

> An odor from a star
> Comes to my fancy, slight,
> Tenderly spiced and gay,
> As if a seraph's hand
> Unloosed the fragrant silks
> Of some sultana, bright
> In her soft sky. And pure
> It is, and excellent,
> As if a seraph's blue
> Fell, as a shadow falls,
> And his warm body shed
> Sweet exhalations, void
> Of our despised decay.

may well have seemed as original and daring as the ironic
pastiche of "On an Old Guitar" (the tailpiece to "Carnet de
Voyage"):

> It was a simple thing
> For her to sit and sing
> "Hey nonino!"
>
> This year and that befell,
> (Time saw and Time can tell),
> With a hey and a ho—
>
> Under the peach-tree, play
> Such mockery away,
> Hey nonino!

Both poems struck poses more self-consciously than the
"June Book" pieces; and in their separate attitudes the critic
can see inklings of things to come—the "old seraph" of "Notes
toward a Supreme Fiction," "The Worms at Heaven's Gate,"
"Farewell without a Guitar," "Le Monocle de Mon Oncle"—
and evidence of images and ideas picked up from Mallarmé,
Shakespeare and his own irreverent contemporaries; but such

matters are for the specialist. What strikes one most forcibly is the uncertainty of intention. Taken all together, the poems written between 1907 and 1914 are as miscellaneous a lot as one can imagine, although the "June Book" pieces have more in common: they belonged to that idyllic world "away from this one" in which he and Elsie were to live their private lives, a world he had invented almost more for himself than for her in the fairy tales and romantic fantasies that filled his letters to her during their long courtship. Elsie liked the poems he wrote for her best of all his work; but even before he began writing them, he had concluded that "to practice an art, to need it and to love it, is the quickest way of learning that all happiness lies in one's self, as Omar says it does." Like so many other surviving fragments of his early letters, this one cast a long shadow. In the "Adagia" he said, "The world is myself. Life is myself"; and his claims for poetry as "one of the sanctions of life" came in time to suggest an equally commanding opinion of the poet: an egotism he was at pains to qualify as "indirect," having nothing to do with "awards and honors," but nearly everything with "the power over the mind that lies in the mind itself, the incalculable expanse of the imagination as it reflects itself in us and about us. . . . the precious scope which every poet seeks to achieve as best he can."

But he had no illusions about what he had written so far. Although it was "a great pleasure to be . . . poetical" and to write

> Lo! I behold an orb of silver brightly
> Grow from the fringe of sunset like a dream
> From thought's severe infinitude—

he recognized that his "trifling poesies" were "like the trifling designs one sees on fans." They were keepsakes. Serious as he was about what he was attempting to do, he still had not discovered a subject or a manner of his own, or a poet whose example challenged him to be himself. His designs were as

conventional as Mallarmé's *éventails* were unconventional,
and it would be more than stretching the evidence to see in
them—at least before 1913–14—any definable influence of his
work or his aesthetic. Stevens knew the French poets; he told
Bernard Heringman many years later:

> Mallarmé was a good deal in the air when I was
> much younger. But so were other people, for instance,
> Samain. Verlaine meant a good deal more to me.
> There were many of his lines that I delighted to re-
> peat. But I was never a student of any of these
> poets; they were simply poets and I was the youth-
> ful general reader.

To Hi Simons, who asked about the possible influence on his
work of Mallarmé and others, and who wrote an essay on
"Wallace Stevens and Mallarmé," he replied:

> . . . if I have picked up anything from them, it
> has been unconsciously. It is always possible that,
> where a man's attitude coincides with your own at-
> titude, or accentuates your own attitude, you get a
> great deal from him without any effort. This, in fact,
> is one of the things that makes literature possible.
> However, I don't remember any discussion of French
> poets; at the time when Walter Arensberg was doing
> his translation of L'APRÉS-MIDI D'UN FAUNE I knew
> that he was doing it, and that is about all.

That there were conversations if not discussions about the
French poets other old friends recalled; and the *Letters* provide sufficient evidence of his interest in their work, although
a mere listing of the writers with whom he had at least a
passing acquaintance, in the original or in translation, makes
it unlikely that he owed more to one than to another. Much
that came from the French, at least before 1923, came by
such "coincidence," or, as he told René Taupin; "*La legereté,
la grace, le son et la couleur de français ont eu sur moi une
influence indéniable et une influence precieuse,*" in other

words, from the language itself rather than from the aesthetic
or the example of any particular poet. The *Letters* also make
clear that Joachim du Bellay, Chénier, Keats, Laurence Binyon,
and even nineteenth-century German painting meant more to
him than the Symbolists before 1914; and his translation of
one of du Bellay's sonnets was undertaken as much for its
subject—a longing for home—as for any other reason. The excitement and examples he needed came after the founding of
Poetry in 1912 and the Armory Show a year later. Even then,
he pursued and continued to pursue his own interests in his
own way. He did not share Arensberg's enthusiasm for Duchamp's "Nude Descending a Staircase" any more than he
admired the "old gold, old rose, boudoir blue, and so on" of
Rockwell Kent's Alaska paintings. He preferred his solitude,
his long walks, his casual reading in the New York Public
Library. He took notes on whatever interested him: *Proverbes
Chinois,* collected and translated into French by Paul Perny;
Les Maîtres d'Autrefois, by Eugene Fromentin; *The Principles
and Practice of Art,* by J. D. Harding; *The Chinese Classics,*
by James Legge. He spent many of his weekends reading and
writing, especially in the summer when Elsie returned to
Pennsylvania. But he also saw something of his friends, and
some of their enthusiasm for the new and different must have
proved infectious. Sanborn, Bynner, and Arensberg he saw
most often; and through them he met Walter Pach, with
whom he talked about some of the younger French poets,
Pach's own painting, and that of "the recent French masters";
Carl Zigrosser, from whom Stevens bought his first prints, and
to whom he confessed a "scandalous passion for the etchings
of Canaletto"; and William Ivins, Jr.—all of whom helped to
shape the course of the new art in New York.

Whatever his opinion of his old poems, he looked forward
to the appearance of "Carnet de Voyage." The announcement
in *Poetry* of a prize for a war poem not only intensified his
interest but provided him with a theme. Under the pseudonym
"Peter Parasol," he submitted eleven new poems which ar-
rived so late that Miss Monroe could find room for only four

of them. Stevens did not take the prize, but the editor's enthusiasm encouraged him, and within a month or two he had
sent her another group. These she rejected; they were, she
said, "recondite, erudite, provocatively obscure, with a kind
of modern-gargoyle grin in them—Aubrey Beardsleyish in the
making": a description less appropriate, interestingly enough,
to the poems that have survived from 1905 to 1913 than to
some of the undergraduate pieces. It is likely that the group
included "Cy Est Pourtraicte, Madame Ste Ursule, et Les Unze
Mille Vierges," "Tea," and "Disillusionment of Ten O'Clock,"
all of which appeared in *Rogue,* a Greenwich Village venture
more hospitable than *Poetry* to sophistication; and it probably
included "Dolls" and "Infernale," which Carl Van Vechten
recalled hearing Stevens read at a party at Walter Arensberg's
apartment in 1914. No one, according to Van Vechten, understood "Dolls" or "Infernale"; but everyone except Mrs. Stevens
liked "Cy Est Pourtraicte . . ." She found it, like much that
he was writing, "affected."

Van Vechten's account of this episode, "Rogue Elephant
in Porcelain," published in 1963, is malicious and gossipy;
but it suggests the disparity between the image of the poet
that emerges from the *Letters* and the appearance he pre-
sented to outsiders. Moreover, the essay shows signs of having
been revised long after it was written; its edges, as in other
impressions of Stevens during these years, are blurred. But
there is no doubt that the group associated with *Rogue*—
Allen and Louise Norton, the Arensbergs, Van Vechten and
his wife Fania Marinoff, and Donald Evans, all of whom attended the party at which Stevens's poems formed the en-
tertainment—made the Stevenses uncomfortable. He was far
more sociable than she; but he was seldom at his ease in the
self-consciously urbane and rather elegantly bohemian life
some of the New York group lived, even when he ventured
into it by himself.

Carl Zigrosser recalled that

Stevens was rather secretive in manner. He once

said to me at the Gallery, "Don't tell anybody that
I come in here," and I had the feeling that when he
went out of the gallery door, he glanced up and down
the avenue to make sure that no one caught him in
the act. I suspect that he especially did not want his
business associates to know that he had a taste for
art, even though he did buy a portfolio for one of
them. It could be that the fear of being considered
"bohemian" was genuine at first, but later became a
habit and a kind of pose. There was something precious even then in his slightly affected and sophisticated phraseology. Somehow the word dandiacal
always turns up in my mind to sum up his character
and presence.

Alfred Kreymborg's amiable recollections in *Troubadour*
are limited pretty much to his first meeting with Stevens at
a party given by the Nortons and to his version of how, on
a walk around the city, Stevens surreptitiously gave him the
manuscript of "Peter Quince at the Clavier" for *Others*, with
the proviso that he would not "breathe a word" about it.
Kreymborg also provided a caricature of Stevens in "At the
Sign of the Thumb and Nose," an "unmorality play" included in *Plays for Merry Andrews* (1920) after the *Others*
venture had run its course. The play was dedicated "Al Que
Quiere!"—to him who wants it—appropriating the title of
William Carlos Williams's book of poems, "Sandpapered with
the affection of [the author's] ego . . . for the scratching of
the egos of: Conrad Aiken, Orrick Johns, Carl Sandburg,
Wallace Stevens, William Carlos Williams—in distinction of
and contradistinction to: Jessie Aiken, Grace Johns, Lillian
Sandburg, Elsie Stevens, Florence Williams, Dorothy Kreymborg—whom it may concern!" In this good-natured but rather
heavy-handed literary joke, Stevens as "Fastidious," a poet
"whose intellect is awry," is recognizable in Kreymborg's
obvious parody of the already characteristic diction of the
poems. Stevens did not, apparently, object; but many years
later, in referring to an article commenting on the Stevenses'

friendship with Kreymborg, Elsie said she had hardly known him.

In any case, the battle of *vers libre* and poetic freedom had been won by 1920, at least as far as the poets were concerned. The Stevenses were living in Hartford, and although Stevens had not completely lost touch with New York and literary news and gossip, he had little time for either. His business trips and the invitations of his literary friends took him to the city now and then, where, according to William Carlos Williams, he "really was felt to be one of the gang," although "always in a distant manner, shyly, unwilling to be active or vocal. . . . He was always the well-dressed one, diffident about letting down his hair. Precise when we were sloppy. Drank little . . . But we all knew him, liked him, and admired him." Walter Pach, who saw him "only infrequently" after he moved to Hartford, and who had helped with the design of the set for his last play, "Bowl, Cat and Broomstick," remembered a visit from Stevens when he listened with great interest to the talk of George Vaillant, the anthropologist. For the rest, the memories and anecdotes of those who knew him in New York are equally inconsequential.

His greatest support came from Harriet Monroe, whom he saw on his trips West and once or twice when she came to New York, and who even visited him and Elsie in Hartford, where they seldom had visitors, literary or otherwise. It was to her that he sent "Sunday Morning" sometime before June 1915. It was also to her that he sent forty other poems before the end of 1921, all but five of which she published in *Poetry*. She did not accept "Sunday Morning" in its entirety; but Stevens said he had "no objection to cutting down" so long as the stanzas she liked were printed in the order he suggested, which was "necessary to the idea." To stanzas I, VIII, IV, and V, printed in that order, VII was added by way of a "conclusion"—a peculiar compromise, certainly, for a poem that had been so carefully structured and composed; although Yvor Winters, basing his opinion on the assumption that the eight-stanza original represented a later "expansion" and "dilution" of the poem as it appeared in *Poetry*, reserved his highest praise for the short form. But if Stevens was disappointed to have "Sunday Morning" so edited, he did not say so. It was, as he must have known, his most ambitious and successful achievement to date, one he would not equal until "Le Monocle de Mon Oncle." Yet it was "Peter Quince at the Clavier" rather than "Sunday Morning" which first attracted the attention of his peers and contemporaries: Amy Lowell wrote Alfred Kreymborg to ask, "Who is Mr. Stevens? His things have an extraordinary imaginative tang. That 'Silver Plough-Boy' is quite delightful, though no better than 'Peter Quince at the Clavier'"; William Stanley Braithwaite reprinted it in his *Anthology of Magazine Verse for 1915*. "Sunday Morning" did produce one enthusiastic response from Arthur Davison Ficke, who wrote to Miss Monroe:

> "Sunday Morning" tantalized me with the sense that perhaps it's the most beautiful poem ever written, or perhaps just an incompetent obscurity. Such restraint! Such delicate dignity! And such ambiguity!
> Have you known Stevens? He's a big, slightly fat, awfully competent-looking man. You expect him to roar, but when he speaks there emerges the gravest, softest, most subtly modulated voice I've ever heard —a voice on tiptoe at dawn! A personality beside which all the nice <u>little</u> poets in the world shrink to cheese-mites!

To Ficke must go the honor, such as it is, of having used "ambiguity" first in reference to Stevens. A year later, he was writing about Stevens again, but to a different tune and with Stevens's contributions to *Rogue* and *Others* in mind, when Witter Bynner and he were preparing to spring the *Spectra* hoax on an unsuspecting public. In an unpublished draft of the "preface" to *Spectra*, Ficke wrote:

> Among recent poets, apart from a small clan soon to be heard from, we have noted only one who can

be regarded in any sure sense as a Spectrist. This
one is Wallace Stevens. In his work appears a subtle
but doubtless unconscious application of our method;
and though a certain antiquation of touch prevents
him from being fully classifiable as a Spectrist, it must
be admitted that his work is by implication related
to ours, a fact which we gladly acknowledge.

Stevens was not in on the hoax, as Edwin Arlington Robinson
and George Sterling—both of whom attempted unsuccessfully
to produce Spectrist verses for Bynner and Ficke—had been;
but he did receive a copy of the book. At any rate, Stevens's
first success, whether in *Poetry* or *Others,* did not make things
easier for him. He wrote to Elsie at the end of August 1915:

—Saturday evening I spent at home, writing a little.
I am quite blue about the flimsy little things that I
have done in the month or more you have been
away. They seem so slight and unimportant, considering the time I have spent on them. Yet I am more
interested than ever. I wish that I could give all my
time to the thing, instead of a few hours each evening
when I am often physically and mentally dull. It
takes me so long to get the day out of my mind and
to focus myself on what I am eager to do. It takes
a great deal of thought to come to the points that
concern me—and I am, at best, an erratic and inconsequential thinker.

One can only guess what the "flimsy little things" may
have been. The characterization fits some of the poems he
sent to *Others,* which did not survive his scrutiny a few years
later when he put together the manuscript of *Harmonium.*
But the opportunity to try something more ambitious came
with the announcement, again in *Poetry,* of a new prize con-
test sponsored by the Players' Producing Company for a one-
act play in verse. The result was "Three Travelers Watch a
Sunrise," which took the prize and was published in *Poetry*
in July 1916, and led to a request from Laura Sherry, di-

rector of the Wisconsin Players, for a play for her company. Stevens wrote both "Carlos among the Candles" and "Bowl, Cat and Broomstick" for Mrs. Sherry; and again, Miss Monroe rose to the occasion. She printed "Carlos" with the same enthusiasm she had lavished on "Three Travelers," despite Stevens's offer to let her change her mind following its single abortive performance in New York in October 1917. "Bowl, Cat and Broomstick," also performed on the tour of the Wisconsin Players along with other short plays by Kreymborg, Carl Sandburg, Susan Glaspell, Zona Gale, and Howard Mumford Jones, remained unpublished until 1969.

Most of the time and energy he could spare from business for writing went into the three plays he wrote in 1915–17; but slight as they seem now, they helped him find his own style, and they provided a bonus in a handful of poems, including "Domination of Black," "Six Significant Landscapes," and "The Worms at Heaven's Gate," which were far more substantial than the "flimsy little things" that had occupied him during the summer of 1915. William Carlos Williams, who often helped Kreymborg edit *Others,* pared two of the original "Eight Significant Landscapes" from the group Stevens submitted, and emended the original version of "The Worms at Heaven's Gate" with the exhortation, "For Christ's sake yield to me become great and famous." One other odd and ambitious piece from these months survived in manuscript: "For an Old Woman in a Wig," a long poem (23 stanzas) in terza rima, part of which Williams admired because Stevens had allowed himself "to become fervent for a moment." Nothing, however, came of the attempts to rework the poem: but like other fragments and trial flights, "For an Old Woman in a Wig" reveals something of his rapidly growing mastery of craft and subject matter which might not otherwise be so readily apparent. The poem was clearly intended to celebrate the beauty of earth and the constancy of change, the never-ending cycle in which sea and sky and the seasons abide to give solace to mortal men, but are themselves always new. Deriving from stanza VII of "Sunday Morning," the theme

is developed in a microcosm and parody of *The Divine
Comedy*, its three parts marking a progress from Hell to
an Earthly Paradise. Part I suggests the overwhelming sense
of loss that memory and awareness of the transiency of beauty
inevitably awaken. Part II continues with a recognition of the
"truth" of the maxim as interpreted by the Second Chinese
in "Three Travelers Watch a Sunrise"—that

> When the court knew beauty only
> And in seclusion,
> It had neither love nor wisdom.
> These came through poverty
> And wretchedness,
> Through suffering and pity.
> It is the invasion of humanity
> That counts.

Part III comes to a final reconciliation in the "difficult aper-
ception" of

> The poem of the composition of the whole,
> The composition of blue sea and of green,
> Of blue light and of green, as lesser poems,
> And the miraculous multiplex of lesser poems,
> Not merely into a whole, but a poem of
> The whole, the essential compact of the parts,
> The roundness that pulls tight the final ring . . .

in "A Primitive Like an Orb," the fiction that is yet "the
thing itself," and that makes, momentarily, "life complete in
itself."

Robert Buttel has observed that "For an Old Woman in a
Wig" was an "exercise" in the direction of "Notes Toward a
Supreme Fiction." It was also a link between "Sunday Morn-
ing" and a number of other poems: "Le Monocle de Mon
Oncle," "To a High-Toned Old Christian Woman," "Archi-
tecture," and "Academic Discourse at Havana," all of which

are prefigurations of his most ambitious attempt to write "the great poem of earth." Formally, like other set patterns which he found uncongenial and "tremendously out of place" in his desire to grasp "the real," this experiment in terza rima may well have suggested the possibilities of the tristich, the stanza he made a hallmark of his work, adapting it with great freedom to his own uses in many of the shorter poems of *Harmonium* and *Ideas of Order*, or in the flexible blank verse of his most ambitious later poems, and in the serene pentameter of "Sea Surface Full of Clouds," his purest celebration of the poetry of sea and sky.

He also found time to complete "Primordia," a group of ten poems best described as an up-to-date, modishly avant-garde "Carnet de Voyage" in the freest verse he ever wrote—as sharp a contrast as it is possible to imagine to the blank verse of "Sunday Morning" and the terza rima of "For an Old Woman in a Wig." The group was divided into two units, "In the Northwest" and "In the South," with "To the Roaring Wind" as a tailpiece. He obviously enjoyed writing these Post-Impressionistic essays in local color remembered from his business trips; but he managed the Southern landscape more successfully than he did Minnesota, and he reprinted only three of them ("In the Carolinas," "Indian River," and "To the Roaring Wind") in *Harmonium*. On the whole, "Primordia" was another experiment in manner.

The same may be said of "Lettres d'un Soldat," which he completed in 1917, on one of his rare vacations, when he joined Elsie at Byrdcliffe, in Woodstock, New York, where she spent several summers. This group of "war" poems, originally longer than the thirteen he sent to Miss Monroe, and of which she printed nine after going over them with him and "weeding out the bad ones," was a curious medley. It contained the first examples of poems in the characteristic tristichs, including "The Death of a Soldier," which is possibly the earliest as well as one of the finest and most beautifully sustained, its strongly accented iambs and repeated phrases modulated with as much skill as anything in Eliot, Pound, or

Frost. Curiously enough, he waited until 1931 to include it in the second edition of *Harmonium,* when he also rescued two others from the group (and the still unpublished "Lunar Paraphrase," which Miss Monroe and he had rejected) and from the limbo into which they had fallen. The "Lettres" ran a gamut of free and traditional forms: they included a heroic couplet; a sententiously witty aphorism in couplets; a parody of an army drinking song; and an awkwardly structured monologue—complete with a kind of stage direction intended to be integral to the text—which foreshadowed the series of poems he called "anecdotes" and also looked back to "Infernale," in which he had tried a similar experiment in rhymed quatrains.

One sees in everything he tried between 1914 and 1917 attempts to find that "authentic and fluent speech" he knew he needed, but which he had not yet achieved. The lack of opportunity for sustained effort; the persistent feeling that "manner" was more important than "matter"; the realization that his own interest in poetry was fundamentally different from that of most of his contemporaries; as well as an unresolved diffidence about his fondness for panache and bravura —all added to his dissatisfaction with himself, his work, and his poetic peers. Again and again, he insisted that poetry was for him a kind of "retreat," and that the opinion of others, including the critics, was of no concern to him. But he also recognized the advantages of seeing his poems in print, even though he never sought recognition outside the little magazines. His loyalty to *Poetry* and Miss Monroe testified to his gratitude for her interest and her willingness to let him try a variety of things. Moreover, appearances in *Poetry* counted, even though the editors' catholicity of taste and their hospitality to poets of almost every school and persuasion irritated, even infuriated some members of the avant garde, who were eager to claim Stevens as one of their own. With a few notable exceptions, Stevens was already sending Miss Monroe the poems he liked best. Eventually, they would provide a fair share of the work that established his reputation: "Pecksniffiana," which brought him the Helen Haire Levinson Prize in 1920; and "Sur Ma Guzzla Gracile," a group of twelve published in 1921. "Sunday Morning" was already a matter of record.

How seriously he had come to take his commitment to poetry can be gauged in part by his letter to William Carlos Williams, written sometime after the publication of the latter's *Al Que Quiere!* in 1917. Williams included the letter in the "Prologue" to *Kora in Hell* (1920), where it was prefaced by Stevens's postscript, "I think, after all, I should rather send this than not, although it is quarrelsomely full of my own ideas of discipline."

What strikes me most about the poems themselves is their casual character . . . Personally I have a distaste for miscellany. It is one of the reasons I do not bother about a book myself.

. . . My idea is that in order to carry a thing to the extreme [necessary] to convey it one has to stick to it; . . . Given a fixed point of view, realistic, imagistic or what you will, everything adjusts itself to that point of view; and the process of adjustment is a world in flux, as it should be for a poet. But to fidget with points of view leads always to new beginnings and incessant new beginnings lead to sterility. A single manner or mood thoroughly matured and exploited is that fresh thing . . . etc.

One has to keep looking for poetry as Renoir looked for colors in old walls, wood-work and so on.

Your place is
—among children
Leaping around a dead dog.
A book of that would feed the hungry.

Well a book of poems is a damned serious affair. I am only objecting that a book that contains your particular quality should contain anything else and suggesting that if the quality were carried to a communicable extreme, in intensity and volume, etc. . . .
I see it all over the book, in your landscapes and

portraits, but dissipated and obscured. Bouquets for
brides and Spencerian [sic] compliments for poets . . .
There are very few men who have anything native in
them or for whose work I'd give a Bolshevic [sic]
ruble . . . But I think your tantrums not half mad
enough.

Whether Stevens's "ideas of discipline" are interpreted as
evidence of self-protectiveness, ambition, or good sense and
modesty, he had not written enough to provide the makings
of even the traditional slim volume. Four of the triumphs
on which his popular reputation would rest—"Sunday Morning" "Peter Quince at the Clavier," "Thirteen Ways of Looking at a Blackbird," and "Domination of Black"—were already
behind him; and about a dozen of the other forty-odd pieces
he had completed in four years were successful and characteristic. The rest, as he knew, were apprentice work—fidgeting
with points of view, if not new beginnings—suggesting only
here and there the qualities that had begun to set him apart
from a whole army of aspiring poets who found their way into
Others, Poetry, the *Little Review,* and their more fugitive
contemporaries.

It also seems unlikely that the irony of being regarded as
the peer of younger writers with little more than flash reputations wholly escaped him, although reputation as such did not
concern him. The fact remains, however, that Kreymborg and
Williams and even Harriet Monroe (whom he addressed in
one of his letters as "Chère Alma Mater"), much as they
admired his work, did not see his "particular quality" as
significantly different from that of the self-conscious "mod-
ernists" with whom they themselves and most other com-
mentators on the current literary scene linked his name:
Skipwith Cannell, William Saphier, Orrick Johns, Maxwell
Bodenheim, Mina Loy, and assorted Imagists, Vorticists, and
Futurists.

His last play, "Bowl, Cat and Broomstick," sums up as well
as any work his own opinion of his accomplishment and what

he still had to learn as of 1917. The "point" of the piece
emerges from the discussion—which provides the whole action
—by the three characters who give the play its name, of
what constitutes the proper relation between the chronological
age and the apparent youthfulness of the verse of a poetess
named Claire Dupray, and what the relationship may signify.
Bowl thinks that because she was twenty-two when she wrote
her poems, they must be young and new; but Broomstick
finds in her work an "emotional waste," a "stale monism,"
and a "sophisticated green" that are all "thirty years old at
the least" and might even be said to belong "to the last
century." He concludes that "she is not herself in her day,"
for to be herself she "must be as free from to-day as from
yesterday." She must not be an imitator; imitation is a matter
of convenience, and "convenience is impossible in poetry."
"It is bad enough," Broomstick goes on to say, "that Claire
Dupray imitates at all. But it is fatal that she imitates the
point of view and the feelings of a generation ago. . . . she
is a poetess in the old-maidenly sense of the word," not the
"brilliant and vivid creature" Bowl conceives her to be. She
is, in other words, the kind of poet Stevens had been until
very recently, whose "habits" were "positively lady-like." In
examining the preface to her book, the three friends discover
that her reading had included "the abbot of Bellozane's translation of Plutarch's Lives, Florio's Dictionary, a volume of
Du Bellay"—"Piquant reading for a young poetess," Broomstick remarks; and not a greatly exaggerated parody of some
of Stevens's reading. They also discover that far from being
twenty-two, Claire was forty-six when her poems were published and is now fifty-three. Bowl and Cat are appalled.
"She will love as long as she lives," Cat says; but he damns
all portraits of poets and poetesses, for, having fallen in love
with her portrait (the frontispiece of her book), he cannot
square that image with what he imagines she must have become. It is Cat, too, who confuses what he calls "advanced"
poetry with mere modishness. Broomstick brings the whole
discussion to an end by observing that "One should always

read a preface first." It is easy to understand why Walter
Pach called "Bowl, Cat and Broomstick" a "book review."
But the play is also interesting from another point of view.
Shortly after the publication of "Sur Ma Guzzla Gracile,"
Genevieve Taggard told Stevens that "there was an impression
abroad that the poems were hideous ghosts" of himself; and
in reporting this rumor to Harriet Monroe, he commented,
"It may be." If, as he claimed, all of his poems had "actual
backgrounds," it would hardly be stretching the intention or
meaning of the play to see it as an elaborately contrived bit
of self-examination and self-criticism, a joke that he undoubtedly appreciated better than anyone else. Certainly Carlos, in
"Carlos among the Candles," is a self-caricature: he is described as "an eccentric pedant of about forty," and he is as
fastidiously aesthetic and exquisitely allusive in his speech as
Stevens sometimes appeared to his friends. Bowl, Cat, and
Broomstick are clearly intended to represent three aspects of
a single self. Bowl assumes the appearance and "finical importance" of a self-styled scholar; Cat is the devoted and rather
literal-minded "appreciator" of the arts, in love with the idea
of being artistic; and Broomstick is the sceptic, the man of
good sense. The parodies of his own poems and those of his
contemporaries, disguised as the poems of Claire Dupray, reduce the play almost to the level of aesthetic slapstick, but
they also provided figures for such later poems as "Banal
Sojourn" and "Homunculus et la Belle Étoile," and part of
the gist of "Le Monocle de Mon Oncle" and "The Comedian
as the Letter C." It turns a self-satirizing glance upon the
temptation to make "poems" out of the names of colors, as
he had done after visiting the American Art Galleries to see
the Chinese and Japanese jades and paintings some years before, and also after attending a similar exhibition of tapestries:

I

Pale orange, green and crimson, and
white, and gold and brown.

II

Lapis-lazuli and orange, and opaque green,
fawn-color, black and gold.

It touches on topics that he was to treat at greater length in
much later work: when Broomstick says, "to look at ordinary
things intensely, is not to see things as they are," he prefigures
the concerns of "The Man with the Blue Guitar" and *Parts
of a World*, even though he may also have been echoing
Wordsworth; and in the comment that Claire Dupray's poems
are "imitations of the point of view and the feelings of a
generation ago" is a presentiment of the response to the National Book Award in 1951, and, more pointedly, a passage
in "An Ordinary Evening in New Haven," triggered by a
remark that Bernard Dorival, the Conservateur of the Louvre,
had made impugning Stevens's taste in painting:

It is the window that makes it difficult
To say good-by to the past and to live and be
In the present state of things as, say, to paint

In the present state of painting and not the state
Of thirty years ago. . . .

Finally, like "Three Travelers Watch a Sunrise" and "Carlos
among the Candles," it illustrates his lifelong interest in
aphorisms and proverbs. As early as 1906, he had noted in
his journal that he would like to have a library of such things
as Leopardi's *Pensieri*, Schopenhauer's "psychological observations," Pascal's *Pensées*, La Rochefoucauld's *Maximes;* and
eventually he did have them: books of proverbs and sayings
in many languages, including a superb collection of Alain,
and his own "Adagia." Broomstick is the epigrammatist of the
play in which he appears: "A man with so firm a faith in the
meaning of words should not listen to poetry," he says; and
"It is only the poetess of forty-two that sits for a portrait
covered." "Three Travelers Watch a Sunrise" turns upon a

Chinese maxim. "Carlos among the Candles" is, essentially, a compendium of aesthetic obiter dicta intended to characterize its protagonist.

As a satire on the aesthetic clichés of the moment—whether he was tempted to accept them or not—"Bowl, Cat and Broomstick" is more sophisticated than Kreymborg's "At the Sign of the Thumb and Nose" and the overripe ironies of Van Vechten, the Nortons, and Donald Evans, who wanted to eat their cake and have it, too. But it does not escape preciosity or the consequences of straining too hard for originality; and in so straining, it is both imitative and modish. "It is the explanations of things that we make to ourselves that disclose our character," he said later; "The subjects of one's poems are the symbols of one's self or of one of one's selves." One of his selves was unquestionably attracted by the possibilities which might lie within the Decadent tradition. But he seems also to have learned from his experience, as Broomstick might have said, "It is easier to copy than to think, hence fashion. Besides, a community of originals is not a community."

What he learned from his flirtation with the drama was not only how fatally easy it might be to lose his own identity as an artist, but also how little real talent he had for the genre; and he must have been amused, after the fiasco of the first performance of "Carlos among the Candles," by Laura Sherry's insistence that he might well become the equal of almost every modern dramatist admired by the Little Theatre movement, from Andreyev to Schnitzler, Strindberg, and Yeats. On the other hand, it should be said in fairness that his contribution to the movement compared favorably with the contributions of most of the other writers who tried their hand at plays for the *kammerspielhaus,* as Pierre Loving called it in his "Introduction" to *Fifty Contemporary One-Act Plays,* the only volume to represent Stevens as a dramatist (with "Three Travelers Watch a Sunrise").

However inaccurately his critics and admirers associated him with whatever they regarded as the "new voices" of the day, or "irresponsible vilifiers of the muse" and "anarchistic poetasters," he often found himself in what turned out to be the best of company; but he had not yet made his mark. It was easy, during these years, for readers to confuse him with the Imagists and the Greenwich Village "exquisites"; and because he shied away from controversy and polemic and seemed not at all interested in literary politics, almost all the new "schools" claimed him for themselves. That he neither confirmed nor denied their claims hardly mattered to them or to him, but it did lend support to the widespread rumor that he was not serious about poetry, that he was, in fact, a dilettante. He had no cause to support, no regional allegiance, no intention of making a career of letters. When he moved to Hartford, he withdrew from what his New York friends regarded somewhat provincially as "the center of things." He was willing to answer William Carlos Williams's request for an opinion of *Al Que Quiere!* and permit him to use his statement in *Kora in Hell*, but he was not about to join the debate. For Williams, of course, the cause transcended artistic and personal convictions and considerations; he was committed to the task of spreading the gospel of modernism with an enthusiasm that Stevens never could share. In expressing his disagreement with Stevens's ideas, Williams wrote:

> The imagination goes from one thing to another. Given many things of nearly total divergent natures but possessing one-thousandth part of a quality in common, provided that be new, distinguished, these things belong in an imaginative category and not in a gross natural array. To me this is the gist of the whole matter. It is easy to fall under the spell of a certain mode, especially if it be remote of origin, leaving thus certain of its members essential to a reconstruction of its significance permanently lost in an impenetrable mist of time. But the thing that stands eternally in the way of good writing is always one: the virtual impossibility of lifting to the imagination those things which lie under the direct scrutiny

of the senses, close to the nose. It is this difficulty
that sets a value upon all works of art and makes
them a necessity. The senses witnessing what is immediately before them in detail see a finality which
they cling to in despair, not knowing which way to
turn. Thus the so-called natural or scientific array becomes the walking evil of modern life. He who even
nicks the solidity of this apparition does a piece of
work superior to that of Hercules when he cleaned
the Augean stables.

Despite their apparent agreement about the virtues of the
commonplace, the "things which lie under the direct scrutiny
of the senses, close to the nose," Stevens and Williams were
not in close accord. Williams was already moving in the direction of a poetry which included the vulgarity and social
problems of urban life; Stevens was concentrating his attention on himself and the "casual" aspects of his experience,
"light and color," "the indefinite, the impersonal, atmospheres
and oceans, and, above all, the principle of order," albeit in
a language meant to convey the quality of "the specific,
concrete thing one is keen for." As he wrote to Carl Zigrosser, commenting on Walter Pach's illustration for "Earthy
Anecdote," "I intended something quite concrete: actual ani-
mals, not original chaos." There was, he said, "no symbolism
in the poem," although, he added, there was "a good deal of
theory about it," which he did not explain.

Williams, like Kreymborg and Pound, was an active cam-
paigner against frayed conventions of latter-day Romanticism,
the dullness of the establishment, and the thinner manifestations of a still active *fin de siècle* movement disguised as
novelty; and his irrepressible vigor and polemic energy led
him into encounters that would have distressed Stevens. Not
that Stevens was unsympathetic; but he expressed himself
privately and obliquely, as in a letter to Harriet Monroe,
which began, "As part of the campaign against the horrors
of beauty, I write on this pumpkin-colored paper." As an
enthusiast for the contemporaneous as well as the visibly

modernist, Williams was almost as much interested in the work
of others (even when he disagreed with its aesthetic or form)
as in his own. Like most of his contemporaries—like most
enthusiasts—he sometimes confused the merely modish with
the truly original; and his blind spots were as apparent as
those of anyone else. But he did not pretend to be a critic
or a professional in any sense of the word. If he enjoyed
literary invective, it was in defense of his own way of seeing
things; he never carried it as far as Pound, nor did he hold
his grudges so tenaciously. One has only to recall Pound's
remarks on Frost, made as late as 1931 in the running commentary to *Profile*, and the undiminished bitterness they reflect,
long after the fact, against Frost's having gone his own way as
a poet instead of listening to Pound's advice:

> As a matter of history it should be stated that
> since 1912 Robert Frost had been producing New
> England Eclogues. Sincere, very dull, without tragedy,
> without emotion, without metrical interest, a faith-
> ful record of life without intellectual interest or any
> desire for anything not in it. The work, inferior to
> Crabbe, but infinitely better than fake. A great deal
> of New England life is presumably as Frost records
> it. It is difficult to see how such life differs greatly
> from that of horses and sheep.

Stevens's intolerance was more private and of little or no
interest to students of literary politics. His bons mots were
in the style of "star-spangled Bynner," which he coined at a
party during World War I when Bynner had waxed unduly
patriotic. His opinions and judgments of his contemporaries
were temperate and thoughtful, made with the prudence of
a lawyer, or with a detachment which suggested that he was
not especially interested in their work. At any rate, he found
the idiosyncrasies of poets more enjoyable and interesting at
a distance, and he avoided controversy as much as possible.
Isolated from literary life in Hartford, he occasionally complained of boredom, but the isolation suited him in many
ways.

Yet Hartford, as he knew, was a compromise, although it
meant material success. He told a correspondent in 1937:

> . . . a good many years ago, when I really was a poet
> in the sense that I was all imagination, and so on, I
> deliberately gave up writing poetry because, much as
> I loved it, there were too many other things I wanted
> not to make an effort to have them. I wanted to do
> everything that one wants to do at that age: live in
> a village in France, in a hut in Morocco, or in a
> piano box at Key West. But I didn't like the idea of
> being bedeviled all the time about money and I
> didn't for a moment like the idea of poverty, so I
> went to work like anybody else and kept at it for a
> good many years.

He tried, for the first six or seven years, to be both poet and
businessman, although it meant being a weekend poet—or a
holiday poet, when business trips gave him time between
cases to spend a few days "doing nothing." But he was increasingly troubled by a feeling that he still had much to
learn and could not afford the time to learn it: "One's desires
keep a good way ahead," he told Harriet Monroe just after
he had come to an agreement with Alfred A. Knopf in 1922
for a volume to be called *Harmonium*. And under the vivid
and comic surface of "Le Monocle de Mon Oncle," and the
poems that followed it, lay a scepticism so penetrating that it
seemed to call into question the value of poetry itself. If
business interfered with the writing of poetry, it had other
compensations: in the solitude he enjoyed on days off, or on
his trips South; in the company of Judge Arthur Powell, the
regional legal counsel for the Hartford Accident and Indemnity
Company, with whom he did not discuss literature but basked
instead in the "paradise" of Long Key, a kind of "poetry" he
always thoroughly delighted in. Such jaunts provided an escape
and a retreat almost as satisfying as writing; or so he disciplined
himself to think. He had, by 1922, concluded that "Poetry
is the supreme fiction"; but there were other things he liked

as much: "Rhine wine, blue grapes, good cheese, endive and lots of books, etc., etc.," as he told Henry Church in 1942, shortly after the publication of *Notes toward a Supreme Fiction*. Nor should it be forgotten that in the "Adagia" he said, "Money is a kind of poetry." He would not, perhaps, have said of the businessman what he said of the poet, that he "must put the same degree of intentness into his poetry as, for example, the traveler into his adventure, the painter into his painting," although he did, in fact, put that degree of intentness—or very nearly so—into business for five or six years, between 1924 and 1930.

He had also begun to feel that his extended business trips upset "life at home abominably," and there is little doubt that his preoccupation with poetry, which made him more than willing to stay in Hartford during what might have been vacations, contributed to his growing uneasiness about attempting to make the most of two different ambitions. After 1916, Elsie did not return to Pennsylvania during the summer; and if he brought his poetry home with him as a businessman might bring his work, she could not share in it. The "affectation" she had disliked in his earlier poems had by no means disappeared; to the casual observer, a group of poems like "Pecksniffiana," which represented several months' work, might well have seemed evidence that his dandyism had increased. But he had learned to control and exploit his fondness for the exquisite and the "quick, unaccountable, [and] responsive" in what he had called "real life" in 1900, in a way that had become, for those who knew his work, a true and distinctive style. Yet he wrote to Harriet Monroe in December 1921, that he had been "churning and churning, producing, however, a very rancid butter" and making "life a bore for all and several" for nearly a month, on the poem that eventually became "The Comedian as the Letter C." He very seldom said more than this; nowhere in his letters does one find him complaining that he had no one with whom he could share his interest in poetry. But the published letters to Elsie written between 1916 and 1923 touch as infrequently on poetry as they do on their private life. Occasionally he expressed a wish that she could have accompanied him on a business trip; and he always looked forward to his return to Hartford. The letters are, however, full of excitement about things and places seen—Minneapolis, Oklahoma City, Chattanooga, Miami, Long Key, and Havana (to which he treated himself on a weekend)—and they bear out his statement that he worked hard at getting ahead in business. He was not often bored, except when he had to travel the same route more than once; his eye, like his imagination, as he said, was not likely to be satisfied by the same thing twice. Florida was the exception to this feeling for new places; and it continued to excite his imagination for a long time, although he missed the change of seasons in the far South, and the exhilaration it brought him.

Quite apart trom their biographical interest, the letters, like the early journal, have a good deal to tell about some of the poems; and they should provide a firm anchor for criticism. Not that knowledge of a writer's sources tells all there is to tell; but to ignore the raw materials out of which he creates his artifacts is to run the risk of thinking that a forest can exist without trees and even of mistaking a forest for a meadow. The artifact is or should be the focus of one's interest; but it does not exist in a purely literary context, without reference to anything except other literary artifacts; and about this Stevens was undeniably clear if not absolutely precise and consistent. One thinks, for example, of "Anecdote of the Jar," over which an implausible amount of ink has been spilled in a controversy as to whether Stevens was "on the side of art" or the side of "nature," for "imagination" or for "reality," almost as if the "jar" ("the symbol of imagination") and "Tennessee" ("the symbol of reality") might just as well have been a ketchup bottle and Alaska; and, in some of the more sophisticated readings of the poem, as if the denotation of the words of which it is made—and also the syntax and the structure—were all but irrelevant.

He wrote to Elsie from Chattanooga, "I have always been of two minds about Tennessee. Sometimes I like it and sometimes I loathe it. This time I have seen so little of it, as yet, that I scarcely know what to think. I know well that I love the far South, along the Gulf, but this midway South is an uncertainty." The next day, from Knoxville, he wrote,

> . . . to the South East, one can see the Appalachian Mountains. . . . The Tennessee River makes a great bend through woods and cliffs and hills and on the horizon run the blue ranges of the mountains. I saw no end of irises in people's gardens. There were peonies, tulip-trees, locust trees and an unknown tree, very large and spreading, covered with purple blossoms. . . . I found lots of motherly old hens guiding their broods of ber-bers through the grass, already deep. . . . I feel quite sure that I rather like Knoxville.

But from Elizabethton, there was no view; only vulgarity, sourness, noise, and a lack of sophistication to make him ironic:

> I noticed the other day that O. Henry, in one of his letters, asked, "Is it possible for anything to happen in Nashville?" Certainly not without outside help. This applies to the state as a whole. I have never been so concerned about a place. I begin to think of it as Pope thought of London: as a "dear, damned, distracting place."

Yet he found the noise of a troop train in Johnson City "intoxicating," the "melody" of a woman "with a voice like a trombone" in the hotel room next to his "extraordinarily robust." He had quite obviously mastered the technique of making the best of flowers in tin cans on fifth-story fire escapes.

Here, in any case, are sufficient clues to the origin of the ambiguity of "Anecdote of the Jar," which both pricks the balloon of local pride by suggesting that God's country of Tennessee is "slovenly," and states that man's deformation

of the wilderness—whether with factory chimneys, ugly hotels,
or a jar—is "gray and bare." Between jar and landscape, the
poem makes no choice; each assertion is qualified by a counter-
assertion. If, as he claimed of "Earthy Anecdote," "Anecdote
of the Jar" embodied a "theory," it would seem to be a
demonstration of his idea that "just as objects in nature affect us . . . so, on the other hand, we affect objects in nature,
by projecting our moods, emotions, etc.," on them, as he had
observed to Harriet Monroe in discussing "Three Travelers
Watch a Sunrise," and as he would suggest much later, in
quite different contexts, in "Effects of Analogy" and "The
Realm of Resemblance." Moreover, the ambiguity of his refusal to choose "art" over "nature" penetrates even the structure of the poem: the neat quatrains and subtly manipulated
consonance create an effect of symmetry without actually
adhering to any fixed pattern. The deliberately "commonplace
guise," like the comic magnification of a trivial gesture, is a
disguise, for in professing or seeming to profess that it is a
kind of joke, the poem becomes something more. Finally, it
fulfills the necessary conditions of the anecdote: it is brief,
interesting, suggestive; and it leaves to the reader the task of
interpretation or illumination.

> I placed a jar in Tennessee,
> And round it was, upon a hill.
> It made the slovenly wilderness
> Surround that hill.
>
> The wilderness rose up to it,
> And sprawled around, no longer wild.
> The jar was round upon the ground
> And tall and of a port in air.
>
> It took dominion everywhere.
> The jar was gray and bare.
> It did not give of bird or bush,
> Like nothing else in Tennessee.

However nicely it fits into the endless dialogue devoted to the question of the priority of art as opposed to nature, or vice versa, "Anecdote of the Jar" owes more to the poet's travels in Tennessee than to Wilde's "Decay of Lying" or to Pope or Aristotle. Rather than choosing art or nature, it attempts to get Stevens's perception of Tennessee "right," in all its ambiguity.

The letters and poems seldom complement each other so vividly and clearly. Frequently, the letters provide no more than hints, like the letter to Elsie from Havana, which includes a great deal more than "Academic Discourse at Havana" and at the same time reveals something of the way in which he winnowed and transformed certain impressions from the total experience into the finished poem. Here, as always, the "momentum" of his mind—his imagination—was necessarily "toward abstraction," not only because without selection the poem as artifact cannot exist, but also because it is of the essence of the mind to interpret what it takes in, or at least to make an adjustment to it. The title itself makes clear the difference in scale and intention from that of an "anecdote"; but a comparison of the letter and the poem also confirms the fact that at the base of his poetry lies the conviction expressed in 1943, when he said:

> If we were all alike; if we were millions of people saying do, re, mi in unison, one poet would be enough and Hesiod himself would do very well. Everything he said would be in no need of expounding or would have been expounded long ago. But we are not all alike and everything needs expounding all the time because, as people live and die, each one perceiving life and death for himself, and mostly by and in himself, there develops a curiosity about the perceptions of others. This is what makes it possible to go on saying new things about old things. The fact is that the saying of new things in new ways is grateful to us. If a bootblack says that he was so tired that he lay down like a dog under a tree, he is saying a new thing about an

old thing, in a new way. His new way is not a literary
novelty; it is an unaffected statement of his perception
of the thing.

But it is also true that in the years between 1914 and 1922
he was most interested in his own perceptions, and only after
he had finished "The Comedian as the Letter C" did he begin
to develop an interest in the perceptions of others. In this
respect, the six poems published in the *Dial* in July 1922,
under the collective title "Revue," mark not only the end of
the first stage of his career, but the beginning of another.
"Academic Discourse at Havana," originally written for a
collection of new poems by "various poets," which was to
have been published in 1923 by a bookseller in Cambridge,
belonged, as he seems to have sensed, not in *Harmonium*
(for he omitted it in the second edition in 1931) but in
Ideas of Order. Even then, the figure of the poet which dominates the final section of the poem remained a persona for
himself.

It is not only the poems which are illuminated by the letters. One sees, for example, in his tribute to John Crowe Ransom written in 1948, very much what he must have seen in
Knoxville in 1918: "The town," he had written to Elsie, "is
now about what Reading was twenty or more years ago. There
are a few rich people, but most of them are poor. The farmers
in the market, which I shall walk through in the morning,
are the most extraordinary collection of poor people, living
off the land, to be found in the whole country." The memory
deepened over thirty years, although it was still characteristically of things rather than of people. In accounting for the
way in which "one turns with something like ferocity toward
a land that one loves, to which one is really and essentially
native, to demand that it surrender, reveal, that in itself
which one loves," he could recall the "trivial things [that]
often touch us intensely . . . the sight of an old berry patch,
a new growth in the woods in the spring, the particular
things on display at a farmers' market, as, for example, the

trays of poor apples, the few boxes of black-eyed peas, the bags of dried corn [that] have an emotional power over us that for a moment is more than we can control." Eloquent as his tribute to Ransom is, it tells us more, in some ways, about Stevens than about Ransom, whose gifts as a poet are centered on people.

In his letters to Harriet Monroe, everything centered on poetry, whether Stevens was stating his opinions of his own work or simply trying out his role as poet. He counted on her interest and sympathy; whatever he told her related to poetry and to his poetry in particular, whether it concerned "a beast of a trip" for the company; a summer in Hartford when he and Elsie felt "as dismal as two grave-diggers spending a rainy night in a vault"; the different things on their way to Hartford from Peking (from Miss Monroe's sister), Paris, Geneva, London, or Mexico, that "[would exhaust] the possibilities of life within [his] scope" at the moment, and that included jasmine tea, cigars, Brantome's *Vie des Femmes Galantes*, a copy of *Ulysses*, some "liqueur from Santa Maria Novella," and the candied violets that so much amused William Carlos Williams; or his impressions of Charleston, South Carolina, where Crispin ultimately landed after his voyage to the New World. She was the literary confidante he needed, with whom he could be as expansive as he wished or as reticent as the occasion demanded. He enjoyed visiting the office of *Poetry* when his trips to Chicago allowed him the opportunity to do so; only once, apparently, did his talk overstep the bounds of social propriety—or what he regarded as social propriety—for he wrote to her to apologize for his "gossip about death," a subject, he said, which "absorbed" him but was "more than a thing to think of" for "too many people in the world, vitally involved."

Among the most interesting letters are those relating to his plays. When, for example, he sent her the reviews of "Carlos among the Candles," he wrote:

. . . I am not in the least interested in proving any-

thing to the critics. They were justified—would have
been in saying almost anything. One is tempted to
put the blame on the performance [in which several
pages of the text had been unintentionally omitted].
But the important thing is to learn something. After
raving about the performance, the possibility remains
that there was little or nothing to perform . . A
theatre without action or characters ought to be within the range of human interests. Not as a new thing
—a source of new sensations, purposely, only; but
naturally, normally. Why not? But no, as we say: the
theatre is a definite thing; a play has a form and
requirements, like a sonnet—there must be passion,
development and so on.

Yet he had not been wholly unresponsive to the critics. Ralph
Block, in his review in the *Tribune*, had characterized "Carlos
among the Candles" as "not unlike a combination of Gertrude
Stein's 'In a Department Store' and Henry James's story, 'The
Altar of the Dead,' with a leaning toward the less successful
futurist of the two, Miss Stein," and had gone on to say:

> The process of this kind of entertainment, in analy-
> sis, appears to be to say something that has no mean-
> ing at all with the bearing of significance, recalling
> what Alice said to—was it the Duchess?—about the
> sound and not the sense being most important. And
> yet there appears just enough method in the entire
> madness of the piece to make me believe that with
> real poetry behind it—such successfully mystic poetry,
> perhaps, as Emerson's "Brahma" or Swinburne's
> "Hertha"—it would yield an entire new crop of sensa-
> tions for the miniature stage.

Lumping together Gertrude Stein and Henry James as "futurists" would have justified Stevens's lack of interest in proving anything to the critics; and the suggestion that "Brahma"
and "Hertha" would provide the poetic force that Stevens's
method lacked must have seemed adequate proof to him that

his intentions had been thoroughly misunderstood. But he did learn something: the three plays taught him "what poetry is, and is not, proper for the theatre," as he confessed eighteen years later, although he also said that he might have done more in the theatre if his experience had not given him "the horrors."

His distaste for miscellany, his uncertainty about being able to "pick a crisp salad from the garbage of the past" when he came to choose the poems for *Harmonium*, like his protestation that publishing a book would "amount to nothing, except that it [might] teach [him] something," found their center in a letter written to Harriet Monroe just before his manuscript went off to New York in 1922:

> I wish that I could put everything else aside and amuse myself on a large scale for a while. One never gets anywhere in writing or thinking or observing unless one can do long stretches at a time. Often I have to let go, in the most insignificant poem, which scarcely serves to remind me of it, the most skyey of skyey sheets. And often when I have a real fury for indulgence I must stint myself. Of course, we must all do the same thing. Ariosto probably felt the same thing about the solid years he spent on Orlando. If farmers had summers ten years long what tomatoes they could grow and if sailors had universal seas what voyages they could take. Only, the reading of these outmoded and debilitated poems does make me wish rather desperately to keep on dabbling and to be as obscure as possible until I have perfected an authentic and fluent speech for myself. By that time I should be like Casanova at Waldheim with nothing to do except to look out of the windows. So that I shall have to swallow the rotten pill.

Of the hundred-odd poems he had published between 1914 and 1922 in *Rogue*, *Others*, *Poetry*, *Soil*, the *Little Review*, the *Modern School*, *Contact*, the *New Republic*, *Broom*, the *Dial*, *Secession*, and the *Measure*—a compendium of the magazines

most influential in the cause of the new poetry—he selected
sixty-seven for inclusion in *Harmonium,* in addition to "The
Comedian as the Letter C" and eight others, two of which
appeared in magazines before the book was published. "Peter
Parasol" and "Buttons" (presumably the poem originally called
"Song"—"There are great things doing . . .") he later rejected
when he went over the proofs. According to Alfred Kreymborg, Stevens had become "bored" with being the only poet
of his generation who had not published a book; but in a
letter to Carl Van Vechten, who was responsible for persuad-
ing Stevens to prepare a manuscript for Knopf, he said he
felt very uncertain about a book. He spent the summer of
1922 on the revision of "From the Journal of Crispin," the
poem he had submitted for the Blindman Prize offered by the
Poetry Society of South Carolina, and to which Amy Lowell
had given first honorable mention; and with the new version
as a centerpiece, it would be possible to make a book that
had coherence and design. Harriet Monroe wanted "The
Comedian as the Letter C" for *Poetry,* and broke the magazine's policy of not soliciting manuscripts by asking for it; but
he put her off with the excuse that Pitts Sanborn had already
asked him for it for the *Measure.* He told her he expected he
would have something to send her "sooner or later," although,
he added, "it takes time and, besides, I have no desire to
write a great deal." His work on "The Comedian as the Letter C" had rewarded him with the unexpected "favors" of a
handful of characteristic pieces, including "Hymn from a
Watermelon Pavilion," "Stars at Tallapoosa," "To the One of
Fictive Music," and "Last Looks at the Lilacs," as well as the
six poems—"Bantams in Pine-Woods," "The Ordinary Women,"
"Frogs Eat Butterflies. Snakes Eat Frogs. Hogs Eat Snakes.
Men Eat Hogs," "A High-Toned Old Christian Woman," "O
Florida, Venereal Soil," and "The Emperor of Ice-Cream"—
with which he made his debut in the *Dial* in July 1922. If
he needed justification for spending his time on a long poem,
to himself if not to "other people," these poems provided
it—"Only it requires a skill in the varying of the serenade,"

he told Harriet Monroe, "that occasionally makes one feel like a Guatemalan when one particularly wants to feel like an Italian."

He had, one would think, adequately prepared himself for almost any sort of reception of his book. But he may also have been preparing himself to give up poetry for a time, even as "a form of retreat," in the pursuit of the "many other things" he wanted enough "to make an effort to have them." Despite his dissatisfaction with what he had accomplished, he perhaps felt that he had exhausted the possibilities of the "single manner or mode" he had struggled to achieve and then to exploit; and his desire to vary his "serenade" suggests that he had discovered that his "fixed point of view" had limitations as well as advantages. To the protagonist of "Tea at the Palaz of Hoon" its possibilities had seemed marvelous:

> I was the world in which I walked, and what I saw
> Or heard or felt came not but from myself;
> And there I found myself more truly and more strange.

His "Nomad Exquisite" had proposed that:

> As the immense dew of Florida
> Brings forth hymn and hymn
> From the beholder,
> . . . .
> And blessed mornings,
> Meet for the eye of the young alligator,
> And lightning colors
> So, in me, come flinging
> Forms, flames, and the flakes of flames.

And the poet of "Bantams in Pine-Woods," having defiantly asserted:

> Fat! Fat! Fat! Fat! I am the personal.
> Your world is you. I am my world.

could say

> An inchling bristles in these pines,
>
> Bristles, and points their Appalachian tangs,
> And fears not portly Azcan nor his hoos.

as if his separateness from the world around him did not matter, since it was he whose imagination gave it meaning. But contrariwise, "The Weeping Burgher" had discovered:

> It is with a strange malice
> That I distort the world.
> . . . .
> . . . I, then, tortured for old speech,
> A white of wildly woven rings;
> I, weeping in a calcined heart,
> My hands such sharp, imagined things.

The poet who cried out, "O Florida, Venereal Soil," had seen

> The dreadful sundry of this world,
> The Cuban, Polodowsky,
> The Mexican women,
> The negro undertaker
> Killing the time between corpses
> Fishing for crayfish . . .

and had sought the retreat of

> the nights,
> In the porches of Key West,
> Behind the bougainvilleas,
> After the guitar is asleep . . .

Crispin, who had embarked on what was to be a voyage across "universal seas" in search of "a new intelligence," had, finally, contented himself with a doctrine that left him, if not where he had begun precisely, then with the world as he had found it, in which poems were "incidental" to its quickness, unaccountability, and responsiveness:

> The world, a turnip once so readily plucked,
> Sacked up and carried overseas, daubed out
> Of its ancient purple, pruned to the fertile main,
> And sown again by the stiffest realist,
> Came reproduced in purple, family font,
> The same insoluble lump.

And, most bitterly disenchanted of all, "The Man Whose Pharynx Was Bad" had concluded:

> The time of year has grown indifferent.
> Mildew of summer and the deepening snow
> Are both alike in the routine I know.
> I am too dumbly in my being pent.
>
> The wind attendant on the solstices
> Blows on the shutters of the metropoles,
> Stirring no poet in his sleep, and tolls
> The grand ideas of the villages.
>
> The malady of the quotidian . . .
> Perhaps if summer ever came to rest°
> And lengthened, deepened, comforted, caressed
> Through days like oceans in obsidian
>
> Horizons, full of night's midsummer blaze;
> Perhaps, if winter once could penetrate
> Through all its purples to the final slate,
> Persisting bleakly in an icy haze,

°This line and the next three appeared in the *New Republic* (September 14, 1921) version of the poem but were omitted in the second edition of *Harmonium* and all future reprintings of the poem.

One might in turn become less diffident,
Out of such mildew plucking neater mould
And spouting new orations of the cold.
One might. One might. But time will not relent.

The arrangement of the poems in *Harmonium* emphasized
both the "essential gaudiness" of his poetry and its "single
point of view," although it did not altogether hide the qualify-
ing ambiguity or the growing scepticism which tempered the
tone of the poems that followed "The Comedian as the Letter C." One suspects that he omitted "The Man Whose Pharynx
Was Bad" not only because he felt that its melancholy would
have been too obvious in the context of the other poems, but
also because its traditional structure seemed to him atypical
of what he had been doing. He later remembered, ". . . when
Harmonium was in the making there was a time when I liked
the idea of images and images alone, or images and the music
of poetry together. I then believed in *pure poetry*, as it was
called." Pure poetry continued to be what he believed in,
even in 1935, when he was faced with the Marxist criticism
of *Ideas of Order*, and he was trying to explain to himself
as much as to his publisher how and why the tone and character of his poetry had changed. And even though one can
think of *Ideas of Order*, "Owl's Clover," and *Parts of a World*
as a departure from the pure poetry of *Harmonium*, the
range of his work was already by 1922 considerably wider
than his statement implied. He wanted *Harmonium* to be all
of a piece; and if "The Comedian as the Letter C" was to be
interpreted as a farewell to poetry, or as poetic autobiography, he was not about to make the announcement public.
He put his long poem in the middle of the book. Moreover,
even if he was giving up poetry for a time, he planned to
return to it. "The Comedian as the Letter C" was an *au
revoir*, not an *adieu*. That this was so, his second thought about
the title of *Harmonium* indicates. He wrote to Mr. Knopf
in March 1923:

I think that the following:

THE GRAND POEM:
PRELIMINARY MINUTIAE

would be a better title for my book than its present
one. It has a good deal more pep to it. If you agree,
won't you change the title for me?

Whatever his ambitions for the future may have been, "The
Grand Poem" would have seemed to most readers the most
private of his jokes. Fortunately, Knopf did not agree. Nor
did he agree thirty-one years later, when Stevens suggested
"The Whole of Harmonium" as the title of his *Collected
Poems*, a choice that echoed the "Introduction" to *The Necessary Angel*, with its apology for his failure to realize the
"ardent" and "excited" ambitions he had once held for a
"theory of poetry."

Harmonium was published in September 1923, and although
Stevens's worst expectations were not fulfilled, it did, in a
sense, "prove nothing." There were not many reviews, but
Marianne Moore's "Well Moused, Lion," in the *Dial*, was both
handsome and perceptive; Harriet Monroe's encomium in *Poetry*, a tribute to one of her proudest discoveries, came a
few months after an enthusiastic review by Marjorie Allen Seif-
fert. John Gould Fletcher was uneasy about Stevens's aestheticism; Edmund Wilson found him "impervious to life." Later
critics, writing with the advantage of hindsight, have found it
easy to belittle these early responses to his book; but in their
determination to treat Stevens with the respect they believe he
deserves, they have been equally guilty of finding in his "preliminary minutiae" far more than is there. To subject everything that he wrote to a kind of analysis which assumes that
his work represents a closed and self-contained, wholly consistent embodiment of a fully realized "theory of poetry," is
to distort and misrepresent the value of his achievement and
the individual poems themselves. Like every other poet, he
had his successes and his failures; and by his own admission,

his "theory" was likely to change from poem to poem. What the early reviewers of *Harmonium*, including those who did not admire it, found in the book, was there—even though it contained more than they saw. How much the reviews were responsible for the financial failure of the book cannot be measured; but *Harmonium* had to compete in 1923 with *Tulips and Chimneys*, by E. E. Cummings, *King David*, by Stephen Vincent Benét, *The Sardonic Arm*, by Maxwell Bodenheim, *Body of This Death*, by Louise Bogan, *April Twilights*, by Willa Cather, *New Hampshire*, by Robert Frost, *Less Lonely*, by Alfred Kreymborg, *Collected Poems*, by Vachel Lindsay, *The Harp-Weaver*, by Edna St. Vincent Millay, *Roman Bartholow*, by Edwin Arlington Robinson, *Selected Poems*, by George Sterling, and *Roast Leviathan*, by Louis Untermeyer. And if in retrospect, few of these volumes would seem to have offered *Harmonium* serious competition, it does not necessarily follow that everything said about Stevens's book—with the exception of Miss Moore's review—was superficial, irrelevant, and wide of the mark, at least in the context of 1923.

However disappointed he may have been in the reception of his first book, Stevens kept his feelings to himself. He told Harriet Monroe that his "royalties for the first half of 1924 amounted to $6.70." "I shall have to charter a boat," he added, "and take my friends around the world." He and Elsie had, as a matter of fact, left on a cruise for California by way of the Panama Canal in October 1923, before any of the notices of his book appeared; and by the time they returned to Hartford in December, his first "burst" had almost come to an end. "Sea Surface Full of Clouds," a memory of that trip, was published in the *Dial* for July 1924; "Red Loves Kit," an ironic, disaffected love poem, in which another of the "ghosts" of himself was the center of interest, appeared in the *Measure*. His daughter, Holly Bright, was born in August.

Poetry and the *Dial* continued to ask for poems, but there were none to send. Even Louis Untermeyer, whose notice of *Harmonium* had not been flattering, asked for something for his yearly *Miscellany of American Poetry;* and although Stevens had nothing new to send him, "Sea Surface Full of Clouds" appeared in one issue. In 1925, Paul Rosenfeld included an essay on him in *Men Seen—Twenty-Four Modern Authors.* The *Dial* published essays by Gorham Munson and Llewelyn Powys, in addition to Miss Moore's review, within twenty-three months of the publication of *Harmonium,* but not before the book had been remaindered. René Taupin wrote in 1928 to ask about the influence of French on his work. To another critic Stevens sent comments on his interpretations of a handful of poems included in a textbook anthology. When Marc Blitzstein inquired about the possibility of using "Three Travelers Watch a Sunrise" as the libretto for an opera, Stevens asked Miss Monroe to send the young composer a copy of the issue of *Poetry* in which the play appeared, but said nothing about writing poems. A few days later, however, he sent her a fragment he had "jotted down in New York," for her "private library." Yet these were merely straws in the wind; and indeed, when Stevens received notice of Knopf's intention to reissue *Harmonium* in a new edition, he left the task of revising the book unresolved for months. He was doing what he had intended to do: concentrating on business and coping with the responsibility of being "a family man."

HARMONIUM

STEVENS WAS almost forty-four when *Harmonium* was published, and if it contained only the "preliminary minutiae" of his projected "grand poem," it included little that looked like apprentice work or the exercises in texture most poets preserve in first books for sentimental reasons or because they have not yet achieved command of their idiom. Although he did not think of himself as a prolific writer, *Harmonium* was a sizable volume. Its skillful arrangement made a clearly defined development or argument difficult to discover; but both were there and could be traced in a reading that followed the approximate chronological order of the poems.

The first notes struck were witty and decorously irreverent: not only was St. Ursula's "offering" in "Cy Est Pourtraicte, Madame Ste Ursule, et Les Unze Mille Vierges" one of "radishes" as well as "flowers," but the "good Lord" who received it responded with "a subtle quiver,/That was not heavenly love,/Or pity"; and "Peter Quince at the Clavier" yoked together in a manner that must have seemed surprising to its first readers a bumbling carpenter-playwright (out of *A Midsummer Night's Dream*) and an instrument conventionally associated with aristocratic refinement. To what extent Stevens intended to *épater les bourgeois* is difficult to say; but he was familiar with the technique. Some of his undergraduate poems and stories had revealed a flair for assuming odd, original, and superior poses. Something of the same attitude, more knowledgeable and more snobbish, characterized the editorial policies of the little magazines, dedicated exclusively to novelty in the arts, which made their brief but influential appearances in the years following the Armory Show, and with which some of his old Harvard friends who had given him his first encouragement were associated. Although he may have had reservations about their "campaign against the horrors of beauty," he nevertheless gave it a passing allegiance.

But even in "Cy Est Pourtraicte . . ." the coloring—"Blue, gold, pink, and green" and "red and gold"—like the flowers —"marguerite and coquelicot,/And roses/Frail as April snow" —was as fastidiously chosen as that of an illuminated manuscript, and counted as much as the surprising attitude toward God; and the last two lines—"This is not writ/In any book" —by wittily disclaiming either sacred authority or secular source for His unexpectedly human response to His charming saint's "low accord,/Half prayer and half ditty," tempered the irreverence. To the charge of impiety or decadence, Stevens might have replied that he was simply looking at St. Ursula with the same realistic appreciation of her beauty that the mediaeval illuminator of her story in the *Legenda Aurea* had observed; which is not to say that his intention had not been partly to shock, if only by indulging himself in his own "heretical" views of sainthood and godliness.

The attribution of "Peter Quince at the Clavier" to the author of "The most lamentable comedy and most cruel death of Pyramus and Thisby" was an intellectual jest and a defense against the possible if unlikely charge that he had misrepresented the story of Susanna and the elders by making it the subject of a love poem; and it seems plausible to suppose that Stevens was enjoying a private joke that a lawyer's love poetry might be comparable to a carpenter's efforts at tragedy. The "instrumentation" of clavier, viols, horns, tympani, cymbals, and bass, like the anachronistic "Byzantines," has been the subject of considerable comment, and has perplexed and irritated some readers, including those who ought to be distressed by the Englishness of Shakespeare's Greeks in *A Mid-summer Night's Dream* and the chimney pots in *Julius Caesar;* but as a matter of fact, Stevens had not strayed very far from the conventions of an Elizabethan "consort of musicke." As for the anachronism of the Byzantines, he told one corres-pondent, "I hope that that bit of precious pedantry will seem as unimportant to˙you as it does to me." He did, after all, need a rhyme for tambourines. Despite its self-consciousness, the title of the poem is very much to the point; and it pro-vides an almost perfect illustration of the distinction between self-protectiveness and self-defensiveness.

"Disillusionment of Ten O'Clock," which reads like a parody of the more excessive Imagist experiments of the day, exploited the trivial in order to make its point about the dull respect-ability and lack of imagination in contemporary middle-class life; but it also satirized, in its excited extravagance, the pur-suit of esoteric sensations by the self-styled avant garde who were the first to praise it and at whose expense, in part, it was written. Nightgowns in "green,/Or purple with green rings,/Or green with yellow rings . . ./With socks of lace/And beaded ceintures" would have been as vulgarly outrageous and old-fashioned to the Greenwich village "exquisites" of 1915 as the respectable white nightgowns were bourgeois and dull. Their taste ran to Whistler, green orchids, and, in night-gowns, "pale grey chiffon." The "old sailor,/Drunk and asleep in his boots," who "Catches tigers/In red weather" would hardly have been the symbol of a more adventurous past or the good old days Van Vechten or Walter Arensberg would have envisioned; nor would the epitome of their romantic dreams have been "baboons and periwinkles." Considered simply as an aesthetic joke, the poem is more high-spirited and lively, and more tolerant of the commonplace, than the overrefined, privileged perceptions italicized in the poems of Pitts Sanborn, Donald Evans, and Arensberg, whose work Stevens knew and admired with characteristic reservations. The essential difference between their work and his is one of tone: where they are merely effete and dedicated to the pursuit of new sensation for its own sake, deliberately cultivating ironies beyond the grasp of anyone except themselves, he is more open to what he came to call the "casual aspects of experience," and his ironies are turned on himself as often as they are turned on his reader. All their effects seem obviously calculated; his seem improvised or at least more spontaneous and natural. Not that he found their world unattractive; but the detachment and scepticism with which he still viewed his own literary ambition, as well as his determination to make a poetry of his own, kept him from aligning himself with any sect or group. Moreover, he was a part-time poet whose interests were not shared at home.

According to William Carlos Williams, Donald Evans, who was imitating Huysmans's Des Esseintes and Villiers de l'Isle Adam's Axel in his life as much as in his verse, was the poet to whom Stevens was for a time most indebted. Evans is an odd, somewhat neglected, and shadowy figure in American poetry, less significant for what he wrote than what he stood for. In his way, he was as much dedicated to the literary and artistic life as Pound has been, but his interests, like his talent, lacked the dimensions, the intensity, and the substance of Pound's, and he had little about him of the generous entrepreneur. Born in 1884, he was for a time the music critic of the New York *Globe*, and it was through his friendship with Pitts Sanborn that he became a member of the circle that included the Van Vechtens, the Arensbergs, John Quinn, and, however briefly, Stevens. One can see in his poems that combination of the *fin de siècle*, the self-consciously modern, the romantic, the iconoclastic, and the gentlemanly that is imaged in various ways in the protagonists of "The Love Song of J. Alfred Prufrock," "Hugh Selwyn Mauberley," and "Le Monocle de Mon Oncle," and in the shabby and ambiguous artists who appear in certain poems by E. A. Robinson, to whom Evans dedicated three of the poems in *Discords* (1912) and, along with twenty-three other friends, *Two Deaths in the Bronx* (1915). Here and there, the correspondences between his verse and theirs derive from a similarity of diction and mood as well

as from a common subject matter. There is no tangible evidence
of any direct influence either way in the case of Eliot; as for
Robinson, any indebtedness would have been on the side of
Evans, who was fifteen years younger than the author of "Captain Craig" and the sonnets, from which he may well have
learned some valuable lessons. Moreover, the dilemma of the
sensitive, responsive man at odds with a materialistic society
contemptuous of his values and ambitions was a subject to
which a great many poets and novelists were turning their
attention; and whether they had been attracted to it by their
reading of Henry James, Browning, Wilde, and Yeats, or
Flaubert and the Symbolists, or as a result of their own bitter
experience in trying to be heard, the subject was not an original
one. Unlike his more gifted contemporaries, Evans was unable
to break out of the conventional forms he had inherited from
the past. Nor was he able, like Robinson, to bend them to his
own uses. The eye he turned on the American social and
cultural scene was so jaundiced that he saw almost everything
with the same disaffected scorn. He never learned the lessons
that Eliot, Pound, and Stevens learned from their experiments
with Imagism—that "some objects are less susceptible to
metaphor than others," and that "the whole world is less
susceptible to metaphor than a tea-cup is"; nor did he master
the difference beween irony and self-dissolving ambiguity, a
lesson he might have learned from Robinson. Yet Pound has
paid Evans homage in his anthology *Profile* by setting two of
the latter's sardonic war poems beside "Nodier Raconte . . ."
and an excerpt (Section II, Poem II) from "Hugh Selwyn
Mauberley"; and Stevens, as Robert Buttel has convincingly
pointed out, found in Evans's diction a contemporary precedent
for his own astonishing rhetoric.

World War I not only sobered Evans's satirical spirit, but
shattered it; and he committed suicide in 1921. Stevens kept
track of him during the last desolate years through their
mutual friend Pitts Sanborn; and after his death agreed to
write a tribute for a memorial volume planned by Arthur
Davison Ficke. He was, however, uneasy about the project,

and when Sanborn expressed the fear that Ficke's volume would make a "literary caricature" of Evans, wrote Ficke to tell him so, in obvious relief that plans for the book had fallen through. Quite aside from the parallels which can be traced between their verse in a handful of poems—"Le Monocle de Mon Oncle" and "En Monocle"; "Tea" and "Placide Pours Tea"; "To the One of Fictive Music" and "Immortal Maiden-Mother"—Williams's memory that Evans "meant a good deal" to Stevens was undeniably accurate. The close, overwrought and airless atmosphere which permeates Evans's sonnets, however, was as alien to his temperament as the fatuous gallantry of the war poems which offered "beauty" as a weapon with which to destroy the Kaiser, although a kindred preciosity touched some of the poems of "Lettres d'un Soldat."

Whatever Stevens's reservations may have been concerning the artistic ferment in which he found himself in the New York of 1910–15, it had its uses; and his flirtation with the avant garde is certainly easier to understand that his interest in the kind of poetry he had admired only a little earlier. He wrote to Elsie in 1908:

> . . . don't you agree with me that if we could get the Michael Angeloes out of our heads—Shakespeare, Titian, Goethe—all the phenomenal men, we should find a multitude of lesser things (lesser but a multitude) to occupy us? It would be like withdrawing the sun and bringing out innumerable stars. I do not mean that the Michael Angeloes are not what they are—but I like Dr. Campion, I like Verlaine—water-colors, little statues, small thoughts. Let us leave the great things to the professors—substitute for majestic organs, sylvan reeds—such as the shepherds played on under cottage windows—
>
> > In valleys of springs of rivers
> > By Ony and Teme and Clun.

Like other members of his generation, he wanted to avoid

both the extreme of believing that "all the poetry had been written and all the paintings painted," and the equally unsatisfactory extreme of adulating whatever seemed new. He was caught between the glib sophistication of friends who espoused the cause of modernism indiscriminately and without real understanding, and his own unabashed fondness for nature as a romantic retreat. Moreover, he had already sensed that "a truly enlightened mind is all the simpler for being enlightened and thinks, not without a modest sort of irony, that art and life exist to be enjoyed and not to be estimated," as Santayana would put it in *The Genteel Tradition at Bay*. At the same time, he recognized that poets were "the most ferocious" of egoists, and that "intolerance respecting other people's religion is tolerance itself in comparison with intolerance respecting other people's art."

He had plenty of confidence in his desire to be a poet, and enough capacity and opportunity for both self-indulgence and the necessary self-discipline to persist in his ambition, however desultorily, until he had proved himself; but neither his confidence nor his attitude toward poetry had much in common with Robinson's, Frost's, or Pound's, nor did he have their temperament for risking everything on a career as a poet. "It is chiefly in dingy attics that one dreams of violet cities," he noted in his journal. Violet cities might be attractive, but they had their limitations. What he needed was confidence in a subject, or rather, a subject in which he could put enough confidence to justify his making the effort to realize it, and a strategy which would free him from conventional constraints. The enthusiasms of his (mostly) younger contemporaries in New York certainly encouraged him to give his own way of seeing the world free rein, to enjoy himself without regard for the conventions of the academy; his own scepticism and detachment—his own egotism—saved him from falling prey to their dogmas. Evans, the Imagists, and the *vers librists* "influenced" him chiefly by enlarging his sense of the relationship between content and form and style; and the same may be said of Laforgue and Mallarmé (among others), whose "discoveries" had become common property among the younger poets of the early years of the twentieth century, even though they may not have been "understood" in the sense that later critics and literary historians would understand them. No one will ever be sure how many of the admirers and "imitators" of Rimbaud or Léon-Paul Fargue, Verlaine or Apollinaire, whose poems helped set poetry free, knew the work of their masters at second hand or by word of mouth; and although Stevens did read and enjoy French poetry, he did not, like T. S. Eliot, "directly" learn his art from "the study of Laforgue together with the later Elizabethan drama," or the "study" of anyone else.

In this connection, it is worth noting that few other poets can have had so little to say about technique or prosody and metrics. When he wrote in 1919 to Harriet Monroe about three poems he wanted to exclude from "Pecksniffiana," he said,

> Not to provoke, but to stifle, discussion, my reasons are that the element of pastiche present in ["Peter Parasol"] will not be apparent and the poem will go off on its substance and not on its style, that I have not yet learned how to do things like ["Exposition of the Contents of a Cab"] and that I am uncertain about ["Piano Practice at the Academy of the Holy Angels"]—as I recall it, it is cabbage instead of the crisp lettuce intended.

He was even more general in the note he prepared for the *Oxford Anthology of American Literature* twenty years later:

> My intention in poetry is to write poetry: to reach and express that which, without any particular definition, everyone recognizes to be poetry, and to do this because I feel the need of doing it.
> There is such a complete freedom now-a-days in respect to technique that I am rather inclined to disregard form so long as I am free and can express myself freely. I don't know of anything, respecting

form, that makes much difference. The essential thing
in form is to be free in whatever form is used. A
free form does not assure freedom. As a form, it is
just one more form. So that it comes to this, I suppose, that I believe in freedom regardless of form.

And in discussing with Henry Church the possibility of a
Chair of Poetry dedicated to a study of the "theory of poetry,"
he was at some pains to point out that he did not mean "one
more *Ars Poetica* having to do . . . with the techniques of
poetry and perhaps with its history."

He did not use the word *strategy* to describe the method
of procedure and technique he was looking for. He preferred
theory, which squared with the "momentum" of his mind
toward "abstraction," and which his training as a lawyer did
far more to sharpen than his exposure to the Cubists or the
"theories" of Mallarmé. The word itself appears for the first
time as the title of a poem he contributed to *Others for 1917*,
a symmetrically arranged bit of "argument" that is both an
artifact and a commentary on the practice of the Imagists:

> I am what is around me.
>
> Women understand this.
> One is not duchess
> A hundred yards from a carriage.
>
> These, then, are portraits:
> A black vestibule;
> A high bed sheltered by curtains.
>
> These are merely instances.

"Instances" equals "illustrations"; and if they "prove" nothing,
they are evidence in support of the original proposition, so
arranged that premise and conclusion interpenetrate and become interdependent.

Warren Ramsey has called attention to the affectation of the French style ("One is not duchess"); and granting the accuracy of his observation, it seems equally important to point out how similar the "argument" of the poem is to Bergson's idea that a character may be described in terms of his surroundings. That Stevens had been familiar with Bergson's writings since his undergraduate days, and had made their acquaintance through the recommendation of Santayana, who knew and admired them, is more than likely; at least he did not deny the accusation that he had founded his view of philosophy on William James and Bergson (and, he might have added, Santayana himself). Bergson's essay on *Laughter* would have appealed to his own temperament; it certainly suited his demand for a means by which to indulge his own imagination and perceptions without falling into the clichés of a modish and intolerant modernism or the morass of subjectivity. Carlos, in "Carlos among the Candles," is an almost perfect illustration of one of Bergson's comic types—the character conceived as the embodiment of a particular "vice" or quality with which "the spectators [acquire] such a degree of intimacy, that in the end [they] get hold of some of the strings of the marionette with which [the comic poet] is playing, and actually work them [themselves]"—which, as Bergson comments, explains part of the pleasure the audience feels. Everything has been so arranged that the audience feels free to interpret for itself; and as Stevens observed more than once to correspondents who asked him for confirmation of their readings of his poems, the fact that their interpretations were not precisely what he had meant did not destroy the meanings they had discovered as meanings.

Bergson raises the social implications of comedy to a level of greater significance than Stevens ever does: for him, truth, vice, and virtue are moral terms which Stevens regards as irrelevant to "the morality of the right sensation." But his recognition of the fact that "the comic does not exist outside the pale of what is strictly human," like his understanding that "a landscape may be beautiful, charming and sublime, or insignificant and ugly" but "never laughable," must have seemed to Stevens a reflection of his own ideas. The ."Six Significant Landscapes" are exercises that illustrate and support at least one of the propositions on which all three of the plays are founded—that "just as objects in nature affect us . . . so, on the other hand, we affect objects in nature by projecting our moods, emotions, etc."—which is Bergsonian enough in any case; and for one of them, Bergson seems to have supplied the essential metaphor. "You may laugh," Bergson says, "at a hat, but what you are making fun of . . . is not the piece of felt or straw, but the shape that men have given it, the human caprice whose mould it has assumed." In the sixth of his "Landscapes," Stevens observes:

> Rationalists, wearing square hats,
> Think, in square rooms,
> Looking at the floor,
> Looking at the ceiling.
> They confine themselves
> To right-angled triangles.
> If they tried rhomboids,
> Cones, waving lines, ellipses—
> As, for example, the ellipse of the half-moon—
> Rationalists would wear sombreros.

The deliberately expository manner gives the poem the quality of a put-on; but it also provides the poet with a means for satisfying his fondness for "little things" and "small thoughts" without falling into the Imagists' error of regarding all objects as "equal." Bergson, early in his essay, says ". . . give your sympathy its widest expansion: as though at the touch of a fairy wand you will see the flimsiest of objects assume importance, and a gloomy hue spread over everything. Now step aside, look upon life as a disinterested spectator: many a drama will turn into a comedy." Stevens, of course, did not need Bergson to tell him that "Clothes make the man," or that a distorting mirror creates comic effects; nevertheless, *Laughter* gave him some ideas and procedures.

The method of "stepping aside" worked with great success in many of the poems in *Harmonium,* and most notably in the long poems that would otherwise have lost their buoyancy and verve. Without its saving detachment, "Sunday Morning" would have been one more cry of despair, and "Le Monocle de Mon Oncle" would have dissolved into bathos. As for "The Comedian as the Letter C," it would have been irreparably damaged; and without the "transposition" of "the natural expression" of its material into an unexpected key, it would have suffered all the consequences of a true confession. Stepping aside also allowed Stevens to concentrate his attention on "the excitement of suave sounds" and "an excitement, an insistent provocation in the strange cacophonies of words" —in "Le Monocle de Mon Oncle," as well as "the sounds of the letter C" in "The Comedian . . ."—and thus helped him vary his tune and, in turn, his meaning. Moreover, the danger of the commonplace as a subject was that it encouraged a poet to be personal and minor; C major was the proper celebratory key, if he could manage it, for a poet whose life was lived "without adventure" but with a sense of satisfaction and fulfillment. One is not surprised, therefore, to find in one of his notebooks the remark that Gounod made of Charpentier, "At last we have a composer who can write in C major."

Laughter is a kind of encyclopedia of comic strategies; and the poems of *Harmonium* illustrate many of them. "The Weeping Burgher," for example, epitomizes the "unsociable" character who "inverts" common sense and spends his time "following up his one idea"; his eccentricity is that of the dreamer who "feels that he has not ceased to be what he is; yet he has become someone else. He is himself and not himself. He hears himself speak and sees himself act, but he feels that some other 'he' has borrowed his body and stolen his voice." Keeping in mind the differences that another occasion and another perspective or point of view necessarily make, one can say the same of such poems as "The Cuban Doctor," "Anecdote of Canna," "Another Weeping Woman," "Palace of the Babies," and the first-person poems in which the speaker is not otherwise identified. Even "The Snow Man" has something of the quality of a serious and elaborate hoax, with his "mind of winter," although the obvious literary analogy would seem to be with sixth stanza of Marvell's "The Garden":

> Mean while the Mind, from pleasure less,
> Withdraws into its happiness:
> The Mind, that Ocean where each kind
> Does straight its own resemblance find;
> Yet it creates, transcending these,
> Far other Worlds, and other Seas;
> Annihilating all that's made
> To a green Thought in a green Shade.

But whether or not he learned his strategy of stepping aside directly from Bergson, he made good use of the technique. It is no accident, perhaps, that "Earthy Anecdote" stands at the beginning of the book, for this was the poem of which he said that it had plenty of theory in it; and in its account of the bucks that "went clattering,/Until they swerved/In a swift, circular line/To the right,/Because of the firecat. . . . Or . . . to the left,/Because of the firecat," he might well have been setting forth in his characteristically oblique way, a key to the fixed point of view that dominates *Harmonium*.

The deepened tone of the later volumes has led his critics to treat *Harmonium* with undue solemnity, as if its high spirits and intellectual play were not evidence of seriousness. But it seems unnecessary to overstate the import of *Harmonium*, which has its unequalled merits, simply to assure its author status as a profound thinker. The astonishing—and appallingly detailed—analysis to which some of these "preliminary minutiae" have been subjected would certainly have perplexed the man who said of poetry that "it must give pleasure." One thinks, for example of "The Snow Man," which has suffered almost as much as "The Emperor of Ice-Cream" and "Anecdote of the Jar" from the devotions of its exegetes. For

such readers, the poem becomes the occasion for an essay on
phenomenology, in which Valéry, Heidegger, Georges Poulet,
Merleau-Ponty, Ramon Fernandez, Santayana, and Bergson,
as well as the total canon of the poetry, are rifled to "prove"
its "viability" and "dimensions," as if anything less would not
do the poem justice. An appreciation of the wittiness of
Stevens's characterization of the snow man as "nothing himself," or of the vividness and accuracy with which the winter
landscape is described, is for them superficial and of very
little significance; yet the poet himself said, "To give a sense
of the freshness or vividness of life is a valid purpose for
poetry," and also, "Accuracy of observation is the equivalent
of accuracy of thinking." For the truly "close" reader, any
analogy drawn between Stevens's poem and Marvell's would
appear to be equally trivial—as the echo in "the sound of the
wind . . . the sound of a few leaves" of Shakespeare's "When
yellow leaves, or none, or few" would seem a mere matter of
coincidence. Yet Shakespeare, not only as "the universal par-
ent," but as a delight and a poet worthy of emulation—particularly the Shakespeare of the comedies—provided Stevens
with a model for some of his finest lines and the figure of
Peter Quince; and "The Virgin Carrying a Lantern" makes
a direct allusion to the passage in *A Midsummer Night's Dream*
in which Theseus, railing against "the lunatic, the lover, and
the poet," concludes:

> Such tricks hath strong imagination,
> That, if it would but apprehend some joy,
> It comprehends some bringer of that joy;
> Or in the night, imagining some fear,
> How easy is a bush supposed a bear!

Stevens writes:

> There are no bears among the roses,
> Only a negress who supposes
> Things false and wrong

About the lantern of the beauty
Who walks there, as a farewell duty,
Walks long and long.

The pity that her pious egress
Should fill the vigil of a negress
With heat so strong!

In *Harmonium,* at least, he took his poetry where he found
it—and he looked for it, "as Renoir looked for colors in old
walls, wood-work and so on," in old books he had liked, in
things that he saw. "Imagination" as "the will of things"
touches this "world in flux" at every turn, beginning even with
"Phases," as the epigraph from Pascal makes clear—for the
sentence occurs in the *Pensées* in the larger context of a discussion of the power of the imagination. The "miscellaneous"
character of his first mature poems—"Cy Est Pourtraicte . . ."
"Peter Quince at the Clavier," "Tea," "Disillusionment of Ten
O'Clock," "Sunday Morning," "Domination of Black," "Thirteen Ways of Looking at a Blackbird," and "Six Significant
Landscapes"—all written before the end of 1917, shows also
that "fashion and snobbery" could be "valuable as a defense
against literary indigestion." Eager as he was to create a
literature of his own, he could not be sure that he should
"not spend [his] time in being modern when there [were] so
many more important things to be," until he had learned how
to let himself go; nor could he say, even on the authority of
Longinus, that the poet "must be contemporaneous" or that
it is "almost inevitable" that "he *is* contemporaneous," with
real authority of his own, until he had learned to distinguish
what was his own from what could be imitated. As for the
Cubists, he wrote to Elsie in 1915, about some of Duchamp's
works he had seen at Arensberg's apartment, "I made very
little out of them. But naturally, without sophistication in that
direction, and with only a very rudimentary feeling about art,
I expect little of myself." He had, however, come a long way
from his earlier enthusiasm for nineteenth-century German

landscapes and farmyard scenes; and his experience with the
new art had helped him to understand more clearly not only
the extent to which his own sensibility, his particular angle
of vision, could be trusted, but that it might contain the seed
of his own originality as a poet. He had begun to grasp the
principle which asserted not only that the thing said was the
thing as said but also that "Things seen are things as seen."

And just as he preferred the word *theory* to *strategy*, he
used the word *pastiche* rather than *imitation*. Following the
"fashion and snobbery" of the moment, at least partway, was
a means of discovering (as W. H. Auden has put it) that
"what needs to be written is the one thing his elders cannot
teach [the poet], just because they are his elders; he can only
learn it from his fellow apprentices with whom he shares
one thing in common, youth." Despite the fact that the imprint
of his character as a poet was visible on almost all of the
poems written and published between 1915 and 1917, they
differed more markedly from each other in manner than most
of what followed. Their virtuosity set them apart from the
models from which they were drawn, but it is hardly surprising that it should be more apparent to us than to his early
readers, who were dazzled by the flashier effects achieved by
Skipwith Cannell, Mina Loy, and Maxwell Bodenheim. Of
those who reviewed the first *Others* anthology, only Conrad
Aiken singled out Stevens and Eliot (who was represented by
"Portrait of a Lady") as the genuine article; and the contributions of Marianne Moore and William Carlos Williams
(including the first and finest version of "Tract") escaped notice
altogether. It was, rather, the specious modernism of Robert
Sanborn and John Rodker, and a handful of *disjecta membra*
by Pound, along with a group by Sandburg and some of Ade-
laide Crapsey's "Cinquains," which received attention. The
accident of their appearance in the same volume gave some
readers the opportunity to compare "Peter Quince at the
Clavier" unfavorably with Miss Crapsey's "Susanna and the
Elders":

"Why do
You thus devise
Evil against her?" "For that
She is beautiful, delicate;
Therefore."

Such was the influence of fashion: the impact of Imagism and the current interest in haiku and tanka, which saw "the delicacy of Basho and Japanese prints" in almost any brief poem that was not in the "Hellenic" mode of H. D. or the "Impressionistic" one of John Gould Fletcher. If Stevens indulged in the exoticism and chinoiserie of the Village exquisites and the Imagists—"Nude porters that glistened in Burma/Defiling from sight," and "Big-bellied ogres curled up in sunlight,/Stuttering dreams . . ."—he learned very quickly to temper such extravagance with something more immediately accessible and native: the "red-bird breasting the orange trees out of the cedars" in "Indian River," the "elephant's-ear in the park/Shrivelled in frost," in "Tea," and the "warty squashes, streaked and rayed," of "Le Monocle de Mon Oncle." Even in "Thirteen Ways of Looking at a Blackbird," where he came as close to haiku and pure Imagism as he was ever to come, the cumulative effect is of something seen and felt, and not simply an imitation of a form.

Like many of his other poems, and certainly his finest poems, the most interesting of these early pieces also strove for "a present perfecting, a satisfaction," not so much "in the irredeemable poverty of life," which it later came to be, as in the power of his own imaginative perception. Yet the longing for permanance and affluence, for something to withstand change and the loss of faith, had already made itself felt; and if his belief that life could be made complete in itself owed most to Santayana, his sense of the impermanence of life and the poignant value it gave to poetry owed more than a little to Pater. On the one hand, the "Conclusion" of *The Renaissance* spoke directly to him:

. . . we have an interval, and then our place knows
us no more. Some spend this interval in listlessness,
some in high passions, the wisest in art and song. For
our one chance is in expanding that interval, in getting as many pulsations as possible into the given time.
High passions give one this quickened sense of life,
ecstasy and sorrow of love, political or religious enthusiasm, or the "enthusiasm of humanity." Only, be
sure it is passion, that it does yield you this fruit of
a quickened, multiplied consciousness. Of this wisdom,
the poetic passion, the desire for beauty, the love of
art for art's sake has most; for art comes to you professing frankly to give nothing but the highest quality
to your moments as they pass, and simply for those
moments' sake.

Yet as early as 1899, he had written in his journal, "Art for
art's sake is both indiscreet and worthless. . . . Art must fit
with other things; it must be part of the system of the world.
And if it finds a place in that system it will likewise find a
ministry and relation that are its proper adjuncts." The difficulty lay not so much in learning to accept the world as it
happened to be—whether the world gave evidence of being
governed by a "system," or was run by chance—as in the
fact that what gave much of the meaning to his life, the power
of his imagination, depended upon the fortuitous, the accidental
aspects of experience. It is no wonder that Pascal fascinated
him, for their problems had much in common.

What was "incalculable" in the practical world posed no
dilemma he could not master to his own satisfaction, although
he "never made that million dollars that [he] started out to
make," as he told a young friend just before his seventy-fifth
birthday. The vicissitudes of the imagination posed another
and less easily resolved problem, and they grew more acute
as his sense of the uniqueness of his imagination became more
and more apparent to him. From one point of view, "The
Comedian as the Letter C" is the anecdote of a man who
makes "life complete in itself" only by giving up poetry; it

is the record of a failure to achieve the ideal set forth by
Santayana in *Poetry and Religion*. From another point of view,
it is the story of a man who is unable to achieve the wisdom
of spending his "interval" in art and song; but its purple,
which is also its wit, is so different from Pater's that it seems
to be a satire of Pater's substance as well as of his style. Certainly the poem is, among other things, concerned "with the
movement, the passage and dissolution of impressions" at
which "analysis leaves off," and it records "that continual
vanishing away, that strange perpetual weaving and unweav-
ing" of the self to which, Pater says, "what is *real* in our life
fines itself down." As a "realist," Crispin chose the purple
of the actual plum, the "good, fat, guzzly fruit," at the expense of the plum "Harlequined and mazily dewed and
mauved/In bloom," and thus steered a course between Cyril's
sentimental fondness for nature, on the one hand, and Vivian's
contempt for it, on the other, in "The Decay of Lying."

Stevens came as close to Pater as he would ever come in
"Tea at the Palaz of Hoon," where his lighter and more high-
spirited comic manner all but disappears:

Not less because in purple I descended
The western day through what you called
The loneliest air, not less was I myself.

What was the ointment sprinkled on my beard?
What were the hymns that buzzed beside my ears?
What was the sea whose tide crept through me there?

Out of my mind the golden ointment rained,
And my ears made the blowing hymns they heard.
I was myself the compass of that sea:

I was the world in which I walked, and what I saw
Or heard or felt came not but from myself;
And there I found myself more truly and more strange.

According to Pater, a poem begins at the moment when "reflection begins to act upon [external] objects" and "they are dissipated under its influence; the cohesive force is suspended like a trick of magic; each object is loosed upon a group of impressions—colour, odour, texture,—in the mind of the observer." And it continues "to dwell on this world . . . of impressions unstable, flickering, inconsistent, which burn and are extinguished with [the] consciousness of them" until "the whole scope of observation is dwarfed to the narrow chamber of the individual mind." Paradoxically, as Pater says, this moment of withdrawal, if it communicates a "sense of the splendour of our experience and of its awful brevity," becomes more significant than "some interest into which we cannot enter, some abstract morality we have not identified with ourselves . . ." Certainly Stevens touched the sacerdotal purple and gold with his own irony; and Daniel Fuchs has pointed to the irreverence of the religious atmosphere, the "ointment" and the "hymns," which nevertheless give the poem its opulence as well as its irony. (To those who asked the meaning of "Hoon," Stevens said he could not remember its origin; he thought it meant "everybody, or rather, anybody," or "Who knows?" But it also meant Stevens himself, though he told Norman Holmes Pearson in 1955, "You are right in saying that Hoon is Hoon although it could be that he is the son of old man Hoon. He sounds like a Dutchman. I think the word is probably an automatic cipher for 'the loneliest air,' that is to say, the expanse of sky and space.")

Nor is it surprising to discover, particularly in the earlier poems, an exploration of more familiar and traditional ways of achieving the "present perfecting" he needed. He had prefigured the satisfaction he would come to value most highly in the opening section of "Peter Quince at the Clavier" when he said, "Music is feeling, then, not sound"; and the final stanzas of the poem had resolved the implications of his premise in the paradox of words (sound) tuned by feeling to celebrate mortality:

Beauty is momentary in the mind—
The fitful tracing of a portal;
But in the flesh it is immortal.

The body dies; the body's beauty lives.
So evenings die, in their green going,
A wave interminably flowing.
So gardens die, their meek breath scenting
The cowl of winter, done repenting.
So maidens die, to the auroral
Celebration of a maiden's choral.

Susanna's music touched the bawdy strings
Of those white elders; but, escaping,
Left only Death's ironic scraping.
Now, in its immortality, it plays
On the clear viol of her memory,
And makes a constant sacrament of praise.

The argument, somewhat tempered by the context of the
preceding sections, was not very different from Shakespeare's
in Sonnet LV:

'Gainst death and all oblivious enmity
Shall you pace forth; your praise shall still find room
Even in the eyes of all posterity . . .

despite the fact that for Stevens there would be no "ending
doom" or "judgment."

The recurring cycle of the seasons was, in "Peter Quince
at the Clavier," the stabilizing source, and the equivalent of
poetry or memory given body in song. In "Sunday Morning," the source seemed to be the sun, "Not as a god, but as
a god might be,/Naked among [men] like a savage source"—
but it was "like," and not "the source itself," although he
returned to the idea again and again: the sun was "the idea/Of
this invention, this invented world,/The inconceivable idea"

with which he began "Notes toward a Supreme Fiction";
and it dominated or played a key role in more than a third
of all the poems. Like art, as he had said in the passage from
his journal already referred to, the sun was "part of the system
of the world," but in 1899, taking a phrase from *Poetry and
Religion*, he was more certain that its "use" was "a service, a
food," than he would be again. "The sun," he said then, ". . .
is certainly beautiful and mighty enough to withstand the
trivial adjective artistic. But its beauty is incidental and as-
sists in making agreeable a monotonous machine. . . . What
does not have a kinship, a sympathy, a relation, an inspiration and an indissolubility with our lives ought not, and under
healthy conditions could not have a place in them." If in most
respects he never really violated this conclusion—a favorite
figure for the world and existence was that of the machine—
he was no longer so sure in 1915 that the relationship between
man and nature was truly mutual. Nature existed apart from
man's feeling for it; and it seldom returned his feeling. To
this extent, at least, the doctrine of naturalism had rubbed off
on him. Nevertheless, "Sunday Morning" made clear how
deeply one's sense of oneself and of the world is affected both
by the "old chaos of the sun" in which one lives and by the
"need of some imperishable bliss" to stay the terrors of mortality and mutability; and its eight superb staves extended and
enriched the argument of Wordsworth's sonnet, although without Wordsworth's confidence that "truth fails not." The influence of Shakespeare, Keats, Tennyson, and even Milton on
this most traditionally measured and dignified of his poems,
as well as that of Wordsworth, has been noted before—and
although the substance of "Sunday Morning" was by no means
unique to Wordsworth and Stevens, but has been, in point of
fact, one of the great subjects, the debt to Wordsworth seems
undeniable. There were also other debts—for example, to
Pope in "Le Monocle de Mon Oncle," where the language and
the movement of line lead the reader to expect something
like Pope's devastating wit; but the couplets never really close,
and are limited, with two exceptions, to the first stanza, where

they occur in the last six lines. The sporadic rhyme is equally
unpredictable, but it serves a similar function of heightening
the effect of neatness, sophistication, and aphoristic thought.
As for Whitman, Stevens admitted to having read *Leaves of
Grass*, but he said that as a "figure" Whitman meant nothing
to him, despite his singular appearance in "Like Decorations
in a Nigger Cemetery" later on, and a use of foreign words
that, although more precise than Whitman's, showed the same
pleasure in them for their nuances of sound and color.

In any case, a debt to English poetry was probably in-
escapable. As he was fond of saying about almost all possible
"influences" on his own work, whether English, French, contemporary or old, whatever he had got from anyone else, he
had "picked up unconsciously." It was for that reason, he
said, that he kept away from all poetry except his own, because he feared influence. And yet, as Randall Jarrell said, it
sometimes seems in reading him—not only the poems but also
the *Letters* and *The Necessary Angel* and the other essays—
that he had informed himself of nearly all works of art in
the known world, had heard most of the music and seen nearly all the paintings. What may have been the most direct
debts—to Donald Evans, to Bergson, to Pater, and, above all,
to Santayana—will never, in all likelihood, be determined.
Much of what meant most to him remains unacknowledged,
probably because his sense of identity was so strong that he
took for granted many things about himself that other writers
have had to struggle to realize.

Although his "desires" continued to keep "a good way
ahead" of what he thought he could do, he had reached a
point by the end of 1920 or 1921 at which he felt "an in-
clination to look back as well as forward," as he told Thomas
McGreevy many years later in commenting on the completion
of *The Auroras of Autumn*. "One grows tired of being oneself
and feels the need of renewing all one's thoughts and ways of
thinking. Poetry is like the imagination itself. It is not likely
to be satisfied with the same thing twice." At the moment,
however, he contented himself with transcribing some of the

"Schemata" and "Memorias Antiguas" he had collected on bits of paper. Some of these contained the germs of poems which would in time get themselves written down. One group of "Schemata" ranged from "Twenty quail flying in moonlight," and "A vivid fruit in a vivid atmosphere," to "The grand simplifications" and "Poetry is the supreme fiction" by way of such wisps of matter as "Holly, kingfishers, grapes and cosmos," "Mrs. Bonfanti's cakes," "Mr. Goldsmith's desire to live it out in Guatemala" and "Experiments on Adam." Others included "A Nice Shady Home," "On Being One's Own Native," "The Man Who Wanted to Think of One Thing Only," "The Error of Crispin Approaching the Carolinas," "The Idea of a Colony," "The World without Imagination" and "Book of Moonlight," all of which eventually contributed their share to "The Comedian as the Letter C." About half of these notations grew into poems; some never amounted to anything: "The Dame Who Carried Her Cane in Her Coffin," "Bandits in Plum Thickets," "The Man Who Could Not Sell Even Nectarines." He did not write an "Anecdote of the Commonplace," but he did make a draft of an "Anecdote of the Abnormal":

> He called hydrangeas purple. And they were.
> Not fixed and deadly (like a curving line
> That merely makes a ring).
> It was a purple changeable to see.
> And so hydrangeas came to be.
>
> The common grass is green.
> But there are regions where the grass
> Assumes a pale Italianate sheen—
>
> Is almost Byzantine.
> And there the common grass is never seen.
>
> And in those regions one still feels the rose
> And feels the grass
> Because new colors make new things

And new things make old things again . . .
And so with men.

Crispin-valet, Crispin-saint!
The exhausted realist beholds
His tattered manikin arise,
Tuck in the straw,
And stalk the skies.

It was from this unpromising bit of self-imitation that "The Comedian as the Letter C" seems to have derived.

Poetry was not a source of awards and honors, but the announcement of the Blindman Prize, offered by the Poetry Society of South Carolina for a poem of some length provided Stevens with the impetus he needed: ". . . What's the use of offering prizes," he wrote to Harriet Monroe, "if people don't make an effort to capture them." The first version of the "allegory," as Hi Simons called it in his essay "'The Comedian as the Letter C': Its Sense and Its Significance," has not survived; but how much the early draft would have told us about his method of working, or what it might have proved, one can only guess. Stevens told Simons that his interpretation and reading of the poem was "correct, not only in the main but in particular, and not only correct but keen," adding only two footnotes to the critic's conclusions. Simons identified Stevens's political position as "on the Right," and Stevens agreed, but he went to some lengths to distinguish his "direct interests" from his literary interests, the "new romanticism" that "the world looks forward to" from "the way of all mind . . . from romanticism to realism, to fatalism and then to indifferentism, unless the cycle re-commences and the thing goes from indifferentism back to romanticism all over again." He wanted, in other words, to keep his poetic intentions from being confused with his political convictions. The other footnote concerned the importance of the sounds of the letter C in the poem, of which he said:

You know the old story about St. Francis wearing bells around his ankles so that, as he went about his business, the crickets and so on would get out of his way and not be tramped on. Now, as Crispin moves through the poem, the sounds of the letter C accompany him, as the sounds of the crickets, etc. must have accompanied St. Francis. I don't mean to say that there is an incessant din, but you ought not to be able to read very far in the poem without recognizing what I mean. The sounds of the letter C include all related or derivative sounds. For instance, X. TS and Z. . . . You have to think of this incidentally as you read the poem; you cannot think of it directly. To think of it directly would be like listening to Till Eulenspiegel exclusively for the personal passages. You have to read the poem and hear all this whistling and mocking and stressing and, in a minor way, orchestrating, going on in the background, or, to say it as a lawyer might say it, "in, on or about the words."

"The natural effect," he added, "of the variety of sounds of the letter C is a comic effect. I should like to know whether your ear agrees." Whatever the merits of his hypothesis, the device had obviously helped him control the tonality of the poem; and although it seems as suspect out of context as Edith Sitwell's fascination with "apricot-coloured vowels" and Rimbaud's "Voyelles," which was more hoax than not, like any other device a poet may use to help him realize his intention, its validity depends upon the success with which it is employed. As Stevens later told Renato Poggioli, his Italian translator, the poem "has made its way without reference to the sounds of the letter C."

"The Comedian as the Letter C" hardly requires further analysis, although for the interested reader the resemblances between Crispin and his creator, the probable literary sources of the protagonist of this anecdote of an "every-day man who lives a life without the slightest adventure except that he

lives it in a poetic atmosphere as we all do," and the uses to
which Stevens put what he had learned from Bergson, or
Pater, or even Santayana, reward investigation. But once one
has caught the tone,—both the witty self-ridicule by which
what is said is mocked in the saying, and the extravagant
delight and self-indulgence in the "plush" of his "poetic atmosphere"—most of the difficulties take care of themselves.
That Stevens sustained his high style so successfully through so
long a poem, in spite of a certain amount of strain, is a tribute
to his capacity for making much of little, at least on the literal
level. For the reader to whom the relation of poetry to life
and the role of the artist in society is of paramount importance,
"The Comedian as the Letter C" must take its place with
"The Waste Land" as one of the key works of its time.

Not every reader will accept the constantly shifting point
of view that lies under the surface of the rhetorical style; and
not everyone will find the figure of the poet a plausible or
convincing one on which to hang a consideration of man's
fate. On the other hand, in its affirmation of the power of the
imagination and the possibilities offered by the commonplace—despite Crispin's failure to make the most of them, or
to arrive at a successful reconciliation between his ambitions
and his capacity, between his notion of what the world ought
to be and what it is—"The Comedian as the Letter C" gives
"the morality of the right sensation" something more than an
aesthetic dimension. Crispin, overwhelmed by his desire for
"relentless contact" with his environment, has to settle for
"things as they are"; but Stevens makes it clear that this is
not necessarily the worst of fates—such a conclusion has its
compensations. But to confuse Crispin's failure with Stevens's
own opinion of all he had achieved to date would be to mis-
understand the poem and to make of its allegory no more
than fictionalized autobiography.

Crispin attempts, somewhat unwittingly, to escape the
limits of his sensibility. He tries to search life for "unprece-
dented experiences." A man of fancy, he mistakes fancy for
imagination. It is no wonder, then, that he fails to "master

life." He settles for the plum as "good, fat, guzzly fruit," rather than the fiction of the plum which hangs

> In the sunshine placidly, colored by ground
> Obliquities of those who pass beneath,
> Harlequined and mazily dewed and mauved
> In bloom. . . .

without realizing that both views are "fictions," and that either view may be a "man's unaffected perception of thing," depending on his nature. Yet Crispin does, in his way, come to terms with his own nature. He recognizes his need for something in which to believe and accepts the satisfactions of his poverty without losing his self-respect. If he has learned everything and understood very little, he at least knows the right questions to ask:

> Was he to bray this in profoundest brass
> Arointing his dreams with fugal requiems?
> Was he to company vastest things defunct
> With a blubber of tom-toms harrowing the sky?
> Scrawl a tragedian's testament? Prolong
> His active force in an inactive dirge,
> Which, let the tall musicians call and call,
> Should merely call him dead? Pronounce amen
> Through choirs infolded to the outmost clouds?
> Because he built a cabin who once planned
> Loquacious columns by the ructive sea?
> Because he turned to salad-beds again?
> Jovial Crispin, in calamitous crape?
> Should he lay by the personal and make
> Of his own fate an instance of all fate?
> What is one man among so many men?
> What are so many men in such a world?
> Can one man think one thing and think it long?
> Can one man be one thing and be it long?

And he sees how

The very man despising honest quilts
Lies quilted to his poll in his despite.
For realists, what is is what should be.

He has only his ego—his wit and his senses—to rely on.
He ends where he began, knowing what he knew to begin
with but attempted to deny, that a man cannot violate his
own nature; and the world is what it has always been, a
turnip. The apology with which the poem concludes echoes
the final paragraphs of *The Renaissance* with an irony that
Pater could hardly have foreseen, and with an awareness of
an irony that Bergson seems to have overlooked by asking the
question, "What is the object of art?" in an essay on comedy.
Bergson denies the comedian the status of the true poet. But
the sense of self—the individual way of seeing things which
distinguishes the poet from other men—and self-forgetfulness
that Bergson demands as the necessary prerequisite for poetic
creation present a paradox that could hardly have escaped
Stevens. "However interested a dramatist (*i.e.*, a true poet)
may be in the comic features of human nature, he will hardly
go, I imagine, to the extent of trying to discover his own,"
Bergson says. But for Stevens, "plumbing the depths of his
own nature in so powerful an effort of inner observation,
that he lays hold of the potential in the real, and takes up
what nature has left as a mere outline or sketch in his soul
in order to make of it a finished work of art" leads directly
to a discovery of his own "comic features." Simply to accept Bergson's opinion that the discovery was prima facie
evidence that he was no poet would have been for him un-
thinkable. The "disguised pronunciamento" of the poem is a
categorical denial of Bergson's conclusion; and the poem as
a whole turns the comic strategies set forth in *Laughter*
against their author in such a way as to disprove his conclusion that "if we laugh at [comic sayings or comic char-
acters], we are equally entitled to laugh at their author." It
is also true for Bergson, as for Dr. Johnson, that brevity is
the soul of wit; and if this definition is correct, "The Comedian

as the Letter C" must be reckoned a failure. But as a tour de force, as the demonstration of comic strategies and of an argument turned "against the man who is, or might be, its author, so that he is made to say what he did not mean to say and lets himself be caught . . . in the toils of language," it merits a good deal of praise.

It is a final irony that Crispin's ambition has been to achieve that state of clairvoyance and "immediate communion with things" and with himself which Bergson—like Pater—calls the object of art. Crispin's ego, rather than the need to live with "the acceptance only of the *utilitarian* side of things in order to respond to them by appropriate reactions," defeats him. He is so self-conscious of his own point of view that he never succeeds in loving "colour for colour and form for form," perceiving them "for their own sake and not for his own," and therefore it is never "the inner life of things that he sees appearing through their forms and colours." Crispin's plum, his "good, fat guzzly fruit" which "survives its poems," lacks the particularity of "the thing itself" even more than its imagined counterpart; but in both instances, the plum becomes entangled and confused in the words used to describe it. It becomes a symbol or an emblem. Unlike the pears in a later poem, "Study of Two Pears," the plum is seen too much "as the observer wills." For Crispin, experience remains a means of self-aggrandizement. He has not learned that the poem, not the plum, is the symbol. His natural detachment is not quite sufficient to be characterized as "innate in the structure of sense or consciousness, which at once reveals itself by a virginal manner, so to speak, of seeing, hearing, or thinking." "Were this detachment complete," Bergson goes on to say, "did the soul no longer cleave to action by any of its perceptions, . . . it would perceive all things in their native purity: the forms, colours, sounds of the physical world as well as the subtlest movements of the inner life."

Stevens remained sceptical of the existence of the soul all his life, but in Bergson and Pater he nevertheless found the confirmation of his own desire "to live in the world but out-

side of existing conceptions of it." He was too ambitious and
too practical to be satisfied with waiting for the world "to
arrange itself in a poem." "The Comedian as the Letter C"
gave him an opportunity to take stock of himself, and of two
theories of poetry which had helped him discover one of his
own. Although he would modify and interpret their doctrines
in many ways, he accepted almost unchanged the beliefs that
the wisest men spend their "interval" in art and song, and
that "the loftiest ambition of art . . . consists in revealing to
us our nature." The artist who "for a few moments at least
. . . diverts us from the prejudices of form and colour that
come between ourselves and reality" is the artist he hoped to
become; such a poet could give poetry the "bearing" and
"position" he believed it ought to have, and it would also give
the poet himself the position he believed he should hold.
That his writing could provide "a means of wresting convictions of selfhood," as Irving Howe has described it, was
for him of an importance equalled only by the attempt to
reveal "poetry itself, the naked poem, the imagination mani-
festing itself in its domination of words" as the peer of philosophy. "Poetry," he said, "has to be something more than
a conception of the mind. Conceptions are artificial. Perceptions are essential." And despite his preoccupation with
his own perceptions to the exclusion, at times, of those of
anyone else, except insofar as they lent support to his own,
he was neither a solipsist nor quite the "disbeliever in reality"
that he called himself in one of his last poems.

He may have been more self-defensive than he knew when
he told Harriet Monroe that *Harmonium* would "amount to
nothing, except that it [would] teach [him] something," but
he had already learned enough from the "outmoded and
debilitated poems" he had sent to Knopf, to build a future
on; and he would come to see *Harmonium* with more tolerance
and affection in later years. Nothing he would write afterward would achieve the particular comic quality of these
early pieces, but as the tone of the poetry deepened, he
could look back at his first book without embarrassment. Per-

haps the judgment he made in 1950 on Léon-Paul Fargue
came close to the truth about his own accomplishment as he
saw it in 1922:

> All during the autumn I have been reading Fargue.
> . . . I suppose that everyone in Paris knew him.
> Claudine Chonez has written a little book about him
> which I finished yesterday. In substance, she dismisses
> him as of no value although she concedes that he had
> many gifts. She thinks that he was of no value be-
> cause he did not let himself go. This means that he
> remained superficial. He never went to the extremes
> of Rimbaud or Michaux. For my own part, I came to
> about the same result, but for a different reason.
> Chonez makes a great point of this: that the imagina-
> tion is always made active by some contact with re-
> ality. Rimbaud followed the imagination in its own
> right. The trouble with Fargue is that he follows it
> in the right of reality; that is to say, he substituted
> Paris for the imagination. Chonez, who has carefully
> analyzed his work, says that something like 60% of
> his poems are about Paris. Within the range of that
> 60% he very often said extremely perceptive and en-
> chanting things. But, after all, Paris is not the same
> thing as the imagination and it is because Fargue
> failed to see the difference, or failed to make any-
> thing of the difference, that he is not first rate.

"The Comedian as the Letter C" had spelled out the consequences of confusing fancy with imagination and the error
of assuming that either imagination or reality by itself was
sufficient to live by. The poet was, after all, a man with a
monocle: one eye naked to reality, one eye looking at the
world imaginatively. The double view might compose itself
to a single inclusive vision, once he had come to terms with
himself.

III. 1930–1945

EXPLANATIONS of the desert places in a poet's career, including those he makes to himself, are likely to fall somewhat short of the whole truth. They require insight and access to private knowledge generally beyond the grasp of the biographer or critic, even though, as in Stevens's case, his acknowledged reasons for not writing seem to have been premeditated and make sufficiently good sense to be plausible. To the ordinary reader, such matters are not of great import; they concern no one but the poet himself. To others, they may be more rewarding than the work itself: Dr. Johnson, after all, thought the biographical part of literature the most interesting. But that Stevens disliked the idea of poverty; that his preoccupation with poetry had not made things easy at home; that his life as a poet, as he said of Crispin's, "was not a straight course," but was "picking his way in a haphazard manner through a mass of irrelevancies" and so "meant nothing to him, pleasant as it might be," were all facts he acknowledged, despite his profound distaste for explanations to others about his poems, his intentions as a poet, and his recognition that "we are all busy thinking things that nobody ever knows about." It did not seem to him to be a disadvantage to have lived a well-disciplined and conventional life; as for his "double life," it was, he told one correspondent, something that other people talked about. "Is an insurance man supposed to be engaged in the insurance business day and night? Is any man supposed to be engaged in his business to the exclusion of everything else and, if he is, what do people think of him?" he asked; but he also said in "The Noble Rider and the Sound of Words," "We have been assured, by every visitor, that the American businessman is absorbed in his business and there is nothing to be gained by disputing it," as if he had finally recognized that the stereotypes applied to both the poet and the businessman were not to be destroyed in the minds of those who wished to believe them, even though they might not survive any sort of scrutiny. He knew, as Gertrude Stein said of Picasso, that no one can be an artist all the time. If his distaste for the kind of literary gossip that passed for criticism in *View* made him unduly suspicious of interviews, the tone of Charles Henri Ford's version of what he had said makes his later reserve easier to understand. And if he was not justified in his assumption that one did not talk about poetry at the Canoe Club in East Hartford (where he sometimes took fellow poets and literary friends to lunch during the last years of his life) because all the members were businessmen, no one violated it more often than he did.

Yet to serious and sensitive inquiries he was always open. In a comment made in 1928, during his longest abstinence from writing, he said of "To the One of Fictive Music,"

> It is not only children who live in a world of the imagination. All of us do that. But after living there to the degree that a poet does, the desire to get back to the everyday world becomes so keen that one turns away from the imaginative world in a most definite and determined way. Another way of putting it is that, after writing a poem, it is a good thing to walk round the block; after too much midnight, it is pleasant to hear the milkman . . .

"And yet," he added, the point of the poem was that "the imaginative world is the only real world after all." His explanation gave away no secrets, but it made good sense.

According to his daughter Holly, he "spent a good deal of his time listening to the radio and, later, the phonograph . . . He also read a good deal" and became "an avid gardener . . . But apparently it was not a time or an atmosphere conducive to creativity. His energy . . . went largely into his work at the insurance company." A few months after Holly was born, he wrote to Harriet Monroe like any other enthusiastic and delighted father; and to William Carlos Williams, he reported in October 1925,

> I have seen very few littérateurs during the last year or two. Moreover I have read very little and written not at all. The baby has kept us both incredibly busy. True she is not under my jurisdiction and has been as well-behaved as a south-wind yet the fact remains that she dominates the house and that her requirements have to a large extent become our own. I have been moved to the attic, so as to be out of the way, where it ought to be possible for me to smoke and loaf and read and write and sometimes I feel like doing all of these things but, so far, I have always elected to go to bed instead. . . . Of course, I do manage to run through a book now and then for, as the Chinese say, two or three days without study and life loses its savor.

His winter trips to Florida almost sufficed to satisfy his recurrent need for poetry; they were, in their way, the equivalent of Crispin's "yearly sonnet to the spring," even though as early as 1926 he began to find Miami, "which used to seem isolated and a place for exotic hermits . . . a jamboree of hoodlums." But Key West, like other spots, was "still fair" and "the real thing." On a business trip to Jackson, Mississippi, in 1930, he found "the town delightful," the "vistas up and down" the river at Vicksburg "among the finest things of their kind in the country," and the people lacking the "knack of putting themselves across and of throwing the light of truth on themselves." The Georgian spring—"peach trees pink with buds . . . taller and statelier groups of pear trees, white from top to bottom," jonquils, and japonica—which he noted on his way to Florida, gave "none of the feeling of Spring" in Hartford, the change "that ought to go along" with "the end of darkness and of ugliness and . . . a feeling of new life or of old activity of life returned, immense and fecund," which meant so much to him. He saw "a vast amount of nature," which he called his "source of supply," but told Louis Untermeyer he was "obliged to see it at the rate of about six miles an hour, and not even a honey bee could do much business at that gait "

His response to all this did get written down in the poems that came later, culminating in "Sailing after Lunch," "The Idea of Order at Key West," "Some Friends from Pascagoula," and "Farewell to Florida." For the time being, however, if he wrote at all, he did so in "momentary violences." The only poem that can surely be assigned to the years between 1924 and 1929–30 is the slight quasi-satirical bit, "Metropolitan Melancholy." There were undoubtedly a few others. He sent Louis Untermeyer for the fourth revised edition of *Modern American Poetry* the brief and characteristic "Annual Gaiety," very much a midwinter-holiday poem and an invocation to "Père Guzz," who, as *genius loci* of North and South—the sun and leader of his muse—was also one more "ghost of himself." An end-of-winter poem, "The Sun This March," appeared in the *New Republic* in April 1930, the first, perhaps, of a handful of new poems intended for the reissue of *Harmonium*. He told Lincoln Kirstein in July, in response to a request for a poem for the *Hound and Horn,* "I am supposed to be writing poetry this summer: actually, I am doing anything but"; and when, in October, he sent his "new material" off to Knopf, he had no more than five poems to add to the five he had salvaged from the original versions of "Lettres d'un Soldat" (1917), "Sea Surface Full of Clouds" (1923–24), "New England Verses" (1924), "The Man Whose Pharynx Was Bad" (1921), and "The Public Square" (1924). Two of the previously unpublished and therefore

presumably new poems, "The Revolutionists Stop for Orange-
ade" and "Anatomy of Monotony," had a good deal in common with earlier work: the former with "Cortège for Rosenbloom," "The Public Square," and "The Shape of the Coroner"
(which he never included in any of his books, probably because of its similarity to "Cortège for Rosenbloom"); the
latter with "Le Monocle de Mon Oncle," from an earlier
version of which its two eleven-line stanzas may have been
taken. The other three, "Sonatina to Hans Christian," "In
the Clear Season of Grapes," and "Two at Norfolk," all
struck a new note; they were, it seems more than likely,
all that he had managed to complete in the six or seven
months since Knopf had written him expressing the intention
to reprint *Harmonium.* He requested that "The Silver Plough-
Boy," "Exposition of the Contents of a Cab," and "Archi-
tecture" be dropped from the new edition.

He was beginning again, albeit tentatively and with no
great confidence, and with what seems to have been a sense
that his earlier poems were more successful than his new
ones. For the winter 1932 issue of the *Hound and Horn,*
which featured R. P. Blackmur's notable pioneering essay,
"Examples of Wallace Stevens," he managed to produce
"Autumn Refrain." He sent "The Woman Who Blamed Life
on a Spaniard" to *Contempo;* and, after telling Harriet Monroe, "Whatever else I do, I do not write poetry nowadays,"
he sent her "another scrap," "Good Man, Bad Woman," for
Poetry's twentieth anniversary issue—with the additional comment, "If it is of no use, don't hesitate to say so. Of course
I shall be furious. But what of it? The egotism of poets is
disgusting." "The Woman Who Blamed Life on a Spaniard,"
"Good Man, Bad Woman," and the earlier "Red Loves Kit"
(1924) were all improvisations on a single theme, cut from
the same fifteen-line stanza pattern he had used in "Sunday
Morning," but reflecting the attitude of a man even older and
more disillusioned than the protagonist of "Le Monocle de
Mon Oncle," who had been "fairly well along in life, looking
back and talking in a more or less personal way about life."
The sardonic, even abrasive irony of these seven stanzas on

love, very different from the ambiguity of "Peter Quince at the Clavier" and "Le Monocle de Mon Oncle," suggests the possibility that they may originally have been intended as parts of an unfinished whole; but because their bitterness was "personal" in precisely the way he thought poetry ought not to be, he never republished them.

In any case, beginning again was not easy. To Morton Dauwen Zabel, associate editor of *Poetry,* who had written one of the ablest reviews of the new edition of *Harmonium,* he replied in 1933 to a request for new work:

> For some reason I have had a good many requests for poems recently. I have complied with a few of these. The truth is that I am not willing to use unpublished manuscript; moreover I do not much like the new things that I write. Writing again after a discontinuance seems to take one back to the beginning rather than to the point of discontinuance.
>
> Miss Monroe has always been so particularly friendly that I should like to make a fresh effort for her. If I accomplish anything that seems to me worth while, I shall send it to you without further correspondence. But it will be some time before anything of that sort happens.

More than a year and a half later, at the end of October 1934, when Zabel reminded him of his promise, he said:

> What is being published now consists of things more or less improvised. Still, I do keep promises when I definitely give one. I shall really try to do something for you, but I cannot say just when: it certainly won't be for a month or two.

There had been, in the interval, some "improvisations," in addition to other signs of a renewed interest in poetry: ten poems in various little magazines, as well as a contribution to Parker Tyler's stylish but overwrought anthology, *Modern Things;* an answer to an inquiry in Geoffrey Grigson's *New*

Verse; and a preface to the *Collected Poems, 1921–1931* of William Carlos Williams. But earlier the same month he had led off the first issue of *Alcestis* with eight poems, including "The Idea of Order at Key West," "Lions in Sweden," "Evening without Angels," and "A Fish-Scale Sunrise," to which the word *improvised* could hardly be said to apply. "Like Decorations in a Nigger Cemetery," the work he ultimately sent to *Poetry,* was more fragmentary and improvisational than almost anything else he ever published. Its fifty "parts" had mostly been written "on the way to and from the office." The title, which referred "to the litter that one usually finds in a nigger cemetery" was a phrase used by Judge Powell, to whom the poem was dedicated, on a trip to Key West. In spite of its miscellaneous character, it was the longest and most ambitious of his recent efforts, and he undoubtedly knew that Miss Monroe would like it.

The growing reputation of *Harmonium,* the thoughtful and more detached response of á new generation of poets and critics, and the sorting out of the achievements of the writers with whom he had been identified while his first book was in the making, contributed their share to his interest in "beginning again." He was no longer regarded simply as the peer of the already-forgotten poets who had made *Others* one of the liveliest poetry magazines of its day, but as the equal of Marianne Moore and William Carlos Williams (with whom his name would continue to be linked for the rest of his life) and as only less important than Robinson and Frost on the one hand, and Eliot and Pound on the other. For the generation of poets who had begun to make their reputations in the twenties, he was a more considerable figure than Sandburg, Lindsay, Kreymborg, Amy Lowell, H. D., or John Gould Fletcher, who had been widely regarded only a few years before as great innovators; or Ransom and the Fugitives, Aiken, Elinor Wylie, and Edna Millay, whose traditionalism seemed less original and therefore less useful, whatever the quality of their individual talents, to a poet starting out in the mid-twenties. Experiment and novelty were still the order of the day. *Transition* was not only the biggest but the most eclectic of all the experimental magazines, picking up where the *Little Review* left off; and its broad internationalism was genuinely new. The *Criterion* was a different matter; it was dedicated to considerations of the cultural crisis rather than to creative experiment. But even though literary generations overlapped, many of the movers and shakers of the "new poetry" were identified with pre-World War I values and attitudes by the Lost Generation and the generation just too young to have fought in the war. It was quite natural that the authors of "Hugh Selwyn Mauberley" and "The Waste Land" should be more highly regarded by the younger postwar writers than Frost and Robinson or those for whom the war had been no more than an incidental concern. The first edition of *Harmonium* suppressed any reference to the war; and that Crispin had avoided all conflict except with his own ego made him look like anything but an "every-day man." Some of the younger poets acknowledged that there were lessons to be learned from Stevens. Hart Crane, for example, wrote to Gorham Munson in 1919 of "Pecksniffiana," "There is a man whose work makes most of the rest of us quail. His technical subtleties alone provide a great amount of interest. Note the novel rhyme and rhythm effects." Others saw in *Harmonium* something akin to the high-spirited gaiety they were finding in the work of Apollinaire and the Dadaists, or the color and refined sensations of the Symbolists, whom they were discovering for themselves in Paris; but they all had reservations about its fastidiousness —a quality Stevens admittedly tried to achieve, and a word that they were likely to use in discussing the work of Williams and Miss Moore, or, a few years later, John Crowe Ransom, with whom Crane thought Stevens had more than a little in common. They were interested in his craft, not in his substance; and in some respects, craft was the essence of *Harmonium*.

But tastes changed almost as rapidly as poetic generations followed one after another in the late twenties and early thirties. By 1931, the Objectivists were claiming Miss Moore, Williams, and Stevens, as well as Pound and certain poems by Eliot as representative of their own aims and intentions. Parker Tyler, whose aestheticism was as remote from the stirrings of a "proletarian" literature as it was from the less sophisticated ferment of the years 1910–20, included all of these poets and Gertrude Stein and Cummings in an anthology featuring Charles Henri Ford (who could, according to Tyler, "be beautifully startled in the presence of words"), R. E. F. Larsson, and several other young poets, in addition to himself, who saw in surrealism the literature of the future. A whole new crop of little magazines with mutually exclusive editorial policies and points of view, except insofar as they all attacked middlebrow cultural views, sought out the same poets; and Miss Moore, Williams, and Stevens frequently appeared in the company of old-fashioned Southern regionalists or former standbys of the *Dial* and *transition,* as well as such unlikely contributors as Robert Cantwell, Vardis Fisher, Manuel Komroff, Horace Gregory, James T. Farrell, Albert Halper, and almost any of the advanced European poets, from René Daumal to Eluard, as well as a host of young writers who had been born when Imagism was in its first flower—all in a faintly revolutionary or politically liberal context. Whenever Stevens appeared, the contributor's note was likely to read, "Wallace Stevens, as has been said before, is Wallace Stevens."

More important to him than the undiminished support of old admirers or the adulation of the young was the growing security and affluence which allowed him more free time to follow his sharpened interest in poetry. In 1932, he bought a house on Westerly Terrace—"the best thing," he told his old business associate and friend, James A. Powers, "that I have ever done"; and in 1934, he became vice-president of Hartford Accident and Indemnity Company. He had "walked round the block" and "heard the milkman" often enough. One other interest which seemed to accompany his interest in writing began to manifest itself: that of having his friends

abroad do "a little shopping" for him—a Christmas box from
Japan, or "Mandarin Tea, a wooden carving, a piece of
porcelain or one piece of turquoise, one small landscape
painting . . ." from China, not to put "on the mantelpiece,"
but to do him "good." When J. Ronald Lane Latimer, whose
literary ambitions in the midst of the Depression must have
seemed more pretentious than they might to present-day
readers, approached him in 1933 for a contribution to *Alcestis*,
a poetry quarterly intended to be distinguished in typography
and design as well as in its contents, he responded with great
enthusiasm. The project had an elegance and a flair that he
admired. The editor was to be anonymous, and the French-
fold pages would be discreetly handsome. The first issue appeared in October 1934; and although the magazine lasted
only four issues altogether, he contributed thirteen poems,
all but one of which were included in *Ideas of Order*, the
first of Latimer's publications under the imprint of The Alcestis Press, the project which replaced *Alcestis*. In his brief
career as a publisher, Latimer brought out two books by
Williams, and one each by Allen Tate, John Peale Bishop,
Robert Penn Warren, Willard Maas, and Ruth Lechlitner, in
addition to *Ideas of Order* and *Owl's Clover*. He also planned
a series of limited editions of selections from earlier poets,
and proposed that Stevens write an introduction to a volume
of Dowson, which Stevens decided to forego in order to
"concentrate," as he said, on his own poems for a "month
or two," so that he would have a "possible" manuscript to
send for the new poetry series. He had the impetus he
needed; by the end of March 1935, just four months after
Latimer had suggested a book, he sent the manuscript of
Ideas of Order off to New York. Of its thirty-three poems,
all but six or seven must have been written within less than
a year; and of the new ones, more than half were written
between November and March.

He quite consciously tried to "pump up floods of color"
in the new poems; and although he saw that they were "not
particularly warm or high-spirited," he did not fully realize

how different his new poetry was going to be from *Harmonium*. But the diffidence with which he had approached the task of selecting the poems for his first book was gone. Even before he sent Latimer his manuscript, he was thinking about a new poem: Richard Church, poetry editor for J. M. Dent, had written from London at the suggestion of Conrad Aiken, inviting him to write a book-length poem for a new series, and he was already considering ways to meet his contractual obligations to Knopf that would leave him free to submit his still-unwritten poem to Dent. Moreover, he was eager to be published in England. His only publication there, aside from a selection in an anthology Aiken had made for the English market, had been in Harold Monro's *Chapbook,* first in 1920, with a reprint of four stanzas of "Sunday Morning," and then again in 1923, in an "American issue," with a slight bit of preciosity, "Mandolin and Liqueurs." He must have worked rapidly, for the first issue of the *Southern Review* published in July contained "The Old Woman and the Statue," the poem that became Part I of "Owl's Clover." He also wrote a distinguished review of Marianne Moore's *Selected Poems,* originally intended for the *Westminster Magazine,* but published in *Life and Letters To-day,* when the *Westminster* ceased publication. Caught up in more literary ventures than he had undertaken since leaving Harvard, he did not foresee the impending reception of *Ideas of Order* or the effect it would have on him and his work.

The first and most telling review, by Stanley Burnshaw, appeared in the *New Masses* and was only less hard on the new poems than on *Harmonium:* the new book was "the record of a man who, having lost his footing, now scrambles to stand up and keep his balance"; *Harmonium* contained "the kind of verse that people concerned with the murderous world collapse can hardly swallow today except in tiny doses," although Burnshaw recognized that it had already begun to look like one of the classics of its decade. Stevens was more upset than he admitted. He told Latimer that he found the review "most interesting . . . because it placed [him] in a new setting"; but it also triggered the most directly personal response of his career, "Mr. Burnshaw and the Statue" (Part II of "Owl's Clover"), which was also one of the least coherent and most strained flights of rhetoric he ever attempted. It gave him trouble, because, he told Latimer, "having purposely used a good many stock figures"—"lights,/Astral and Shelleyan," "ploughmen, peacocks, doves"—the poem seemed "most un-Burnshawesque."

Friendlier reviews followed, including a notable one by Howard Baker in the *Southern Review*, which Stevens thought came closer to understanding him than anyone else had ever come. But Geoffrey Grigson, writing in *New Verse* under the title "The Stuffed Goldfinch," made a point similar to Burnshaw's with more sophistication and a sharper eye for Stevens's manner:

> *Harmonium* (1923), Mr. Wallace Stevens's only other book of verse, gave him a reputation. There we had a delicate man, an ironist, an imagist, a modern, a thin-fingered undemocratic American. There we had *Peter Quince at the Clavier, Two Figures in Dense Violet Night, The Emperor of Ice-Cream;* and here we have them still. The same titles, *Dance of the Macabre Mice, Lions in Sweden, Botanist on Alp, Evening without Angels*—less panache, periwinkle, cantilene, fewer melons and peacocks, but still the finicking privateer, prosy Herrick, Klee without rhythm, observing nothing, single artificer of his own world of mannerism, mixer-up of chinoiserie, recollections of light in Claude, sharp sounds in Mozart, trinkets of culture; substituting for Claude's "calm sunshine of the heart" (the human heart and real sunshine) an uneasy subjective twinkle of sequins, describing thirteen ways of seeing a blackbird, forgetting the blackbird. Too much Wallace Stevens, too little everything else. And he knows all this: refer to *Sailing after Lunch,* nearly a good poem, and a confession. . . .—decidedly, this charming Wallace Stevens is fixed in his 1923. He is dated between the

two realities of the past and the future; that means,
he is an "imagist" emanation of a *dies non* we do
not remember and do not bother to recall.

During this time, Stevens had a good deal to say about
the political implications and the "leaning to the left" of
certain poems in *Ideas of Order*, but it was not convincing;
and by the time Knopf published the trade edition of the
book a year later—with "Farewell to Florida," a new poem,
significantly placed at the beginning—he had given up such
illusions. His statement on the jacket was his riposte to his
critics:

> We think of changes occurring today as economic
> changes, involving political and social changes. Such
> changes raise questions of political and social order.
>   While it is inevitable that a poet should be con-
> cerned with such questions, this book, although it
> reflects them, is primarily concerned with ideas of
> order of a different nature, as, for example, the de-
> pendence of the individual, confronting the elimina-
> tion of established ideas, on the general sense of order;
> the idea of order created by individual concepts,
> as of the poet, in "The Idea of Order at Key West";
> the idea of order arising from the practice of any art,
> as of poetry in "Sailing after Lunch."
>   The book is essentially a book of pure poetry. I
> believe that, in any society, the poet should be the
> exponent of the imagination of that society. *Ideas
> of Order* attempts to illustrate the role of the imagi-
> nation in life, and particularly the role of the imagi-
> nation in life at present. The more realistic life may
> be, the more it needs the stimulus of the imagination.

With such a statement one could hardly quarrel, unless one
adhered to the party line of the *New Masses* or was, as Stevens said somewhat unjustly of Grigson, a propagandist and
"a poet just out of school." There was enough truth in the
accusations of both Burnshaw and Grigson to make them more

than merely plausible; and he himself was troubled by the difficulty of making poetry out of what he called "the social situation . . . the most absorbing thing in the world of 1936." He tried to come to grips with the subject—with "what one reads in the newspapers," "Ryan's Lunch," "men in crowds," "The empty spirit/In vacant space," "A dirty house in a gutted world"—and it would compound the errors of Grigson and Burnshaw to regard his "social" poems, including a handful in *Ideas of Order*, "The Men That Are Falling," and some of the poems in *Parts of a World* simply as aberrations in a career devoted only to "pure" or "philosophical" poetry, as some of his more recent critics would have it. Nor can one object to his keeping the world of letters separate from his world of business (and politics) except insofar as it sometimes dehumanized his poetry. He disliked the word "art" almost as much as he disliked "the numerous asses of the first water . . . people who walked round with cigarette holders a foot long and so on," who attended the premiere in Hartford of *Four Saints in Three Acts*. He was both unwilling and unable to ignore the social conventions which sometimes irked him, and frequently exaggerated the importance of appearing to his business colleagues in the role of the successful American, with most if not all of the successful American's prejudices, just as he sometimes intimidated those whose tastes differed from his own with a certitude that was as immodest as that of most other poets and a sense of intellectual privilege reserved for "the anointed," which verged on snobbery. He professed to have little or no use for the figure of the poet as "an idler, a man without clothes, a drunk, etc.," and said that "the people of sound logic" he knew shared his attitude that "the contemporary poet is simply a contemporary man who writes poetry." But he knew very well that the poet was not, as he sometimes liked to insist, "an ordinary man." In his reaction against the popular clichés and stereotypes of the poet, he could not, perhaps, see that he was creating an image equally invalid and atypical. Much as he was dedicated to the belief that the poet was "any man of imagination," and that poetry involved "an interdependence of reality and imagination as equals," his own sense of what constituted that interdependence and equality was so powerful that it often made him intolerant of any other view. As Roy Harvey Pearce has said, "the intelligence" that his poems "resisted" almost too successfully, was his own: "in Stevens' deepest thought, his universe belonged too much to him. And the division was within him, so that he was not divided but dividing." As his thought and poetry matured, he turned more and more to those friends and confidants to whom he could let himself go when he was not writing his poetry, with whom he could carry on the dialogue with himself which, in the poems, represented his effort to "get the world right," or, more precisely, the effort to get his world right. In commenting to Latimer on Howard Baker's review of *Ideas of Order*, he said, ". . . however striking Mr. Baker's analysis may be, what he does not see is the sort of world in which I am living. If I could create an actuality, it would be quite a different world in a good many ways from the world about us"; as for Baker's discussion of "The Comedian as the Letter C," it had concentrated too much attention on the "matter" of the fable at the expense of its "manner," or that aspect of the manner which was most important: Crispin's life had been intended to represent "the sort of life that millions of people live," without any "embellishments" except those Stevens had been "interested in at the moment: words and sounds," as if the words and sounds could somehow be separated from the life. In summing up this brief discussion of "The Comedian as the Letter C" he wrote to Latimer, "I infer that, for you, environment means men and women; but for me, it means my surroundings, not necessarily natural surroundings. It is hard to say what would have happened to Crispin in contact with men and women, not to speak of the present-day unemployed. I think it would have been a catastrophe for him." In the light of this statement it seems clear that Stevens had taken for granted that his readers would see and understand

—be tolerant of and amused by—Crispin's self-evident egotism, and that they would not be put off by the disparity between his sense of his surroundings (of himself) and their own. Taken simply as a character in a poem, acting out his fate against a recognizable background, he should have been perfectly transparent. But what the statement most clearly suggests is that Crispin, his "prismy blonde" and "daughters with curls" were no more than metaphors for the life lived in the mind, creatures descended from those he had invented to occupy that "world away from this one," to which he had been so much attracted before his marriage to Elsie, and which had more than a little in common with the "actuality" he still wanted to create thirty-odd years later, different as it might be "in a good many ways" from the actuality of Westerly Terrace, his office, and Hartford.

Latimer provided the necessary foil for the revaluation of his accomplishments and intentions, at least for a time. Their discussions led back and forth, in and out of politics and poetry, and into indiscretions which later critics may yet use to "prove" their cases against his "thought" with the same distorted perspective that they have used on Yeats and Eliot. The commentary involved, among other subjects, Mussolini and the Ethiopian War—"I am pro-Mussolini, personally. . . . The Italians have as much right to take Ethiopia from the coons as the coons had to take it from the boa-constrictors," an opinion he qualified later by saying, "all my sympathies are the other way: with the coons and boa-constrictors. However," he added, "ought I, as a matter of reason, to have sympathized with the Indians as against the Colonists in this country? . . . that Mussolini is right, practically, has certainly a great deal to be said for it." He may have feared communism more than he feared fascism; but the evidence suggests that political ideology bored him:

> I think we all feel that there is conflict between the
> rise of a lower class with all its realities, and the
> indulgences of an upper class. . . . My conclusion is

that, while there is a conflict, it is not an essential
conflict. The conflict is temporary. The only possible
order of life is one in which all order is incessantly
changing. Marxism may or may not destroy the existing sentiment of the marvellous; if it does, it will
create another. It was a very common fear that So-
cialism would dirty the world; it is an equally common fear that Communism will do the same thing. I
think that this is all nonsense. Of course, that would
be the immediate effect, as any upheaval results in
disorder.

Like most other American poets of his generation, he never
considered politics or the class struggle a subject for poetry;
and he was unprepared to cope with any view of art which
proposed for the poet a social obligation. He had, it is true,
observed in "Academic Discourse at Havana" that "Politic
man ordained/Imagination as the fateful sin," and had expressed a somewhat facile contempt both for "grandmother
and her basketful of pears" as "the crux for our compendia,"
and "the burgher's breast" as "the place for prodigy"; and
in "Botanist on Alp (No. 1)" he had complained that

Panoramas are not what they used to be.
Claude has been dead a long time
And apostrophes are forbidden on the funicular.
Marx has ruined Nature,
For the moment.

not so much with nostalgia for the good old days as with an
insistence that the "panorama of despair/Cannot be the spe-
cialty/Of this ecstatic air." But grandmother and the burgher,
like his botanist and his alp, were emblems of the mind, abstracted and a little thin, not the "specific concrete thing"
he had aimed for and often achieved in *Harmonium*. He
would have agreed with Chekhov that "writers engage in
politics only in so far as it is necessary to defend people
against politics," but it was a necessity he never really recognized and would have modified to read "in so far as it is

necessary to defend themselves against politics." He clung to the belief that as a private citizen his politics might matter a good deal. As a poet he believed that poetry was not and could not be an instrument of political power. The order it created or was intended to create was a purely individual order. Yet "the real trouble with poetry," he told Latimer in 1935, "is that poets have no conception of the importance of the thing. Life without poetry is, in effect, life without a sanction." As a sanction to take the place of a belief in God it was or seemed to be easier to understand and accept than as a political sanction, which threatened his freedom to express himself as he wished to express himself. "The world," he was convinced, "never moves at a very high level, but a few men should always move at a very high level; whether these two levels will ever sufficiently approach each other and poetry again . . . regain its loss, remains to be seen." To work at this high level and at the same time to "stick to the facts" did not, he realized, solve the problem of creating an order which would do for others what poetry did for him, since the "facts" would inevitably be the facts as he saw them.

His refusal to take the attitude of an artist on "bad terms with society" because "his work was not appreciated" saved "Owl's Clover" from the worst excesses of the social and political poetry of the period; and it taught him what Auden said four years later of the "embittered" poet:

> His political thinking cannot be based on an objective view of society from his unique social position *qua* artist—for, in so far as he is unsuccessful, he is, socially speaking, no artist at all, but just a failure, along with all the other failures, with the unemployed, tramps, footpads and prostitutes whom society does not recognize. No, it can be only based upon introspective observation of his own activities, *i.e.*, of the artistic creative process. Now, just as the artist *qua* citizen is the only person for whom society is really open, so *qua* artist, *i.e.*, in relation to what he does, he

is the only person who is really a dictator. Works of
art really are closed societies, and they are made . . .
by the artist alone without any social assistance. Political generalizations, based on the introspection of
artists, will tend therefore to be "idealist" and anti-
democratic . . .

What saved Stevens from an intolerant and undemocratic
idealism was the detachment with which he managed to
observe his own activities, his own "creative process"; for
however one views "Owl's Clover", whether as discourse,
invective, satire, or polemic, and whether one regards its
argument in rhetorical or philosophic terms, he turned as
severe an eye on the poet as he did on his critics:

> Mesdames, one might believe that Shelley lies
> Less in the stars than in their earthy wake,
> Since the radiant disclosures that you make
> Are of an eternal vista, manqué and gold
> And brown, an Italy of the mind, a place
> Of fear before the disorder of the strange,
> A time in which the poets' politics
> Will rule in a poets' world. Yet that will be
> A world impossible for poets, who
> Complain and prophesy, in their complaints,
> And are never of the world in which they live.
> Disclose the rude and ruddy at their jobs
> And if you weep for peacocks that are gone
> Or dance the death of doves, most sallowly,
> Who knows? The ploughman may not live alone
> With his plough, the peacock may abandon pride,
> The dove's adagio may lose its depth
> And change. If ploughmen, peacocks, doves alike
> In vast disorder live in the ruins, free,
> The charts destroyed, even disorder may,
> So seen, have an order of its own, a peace
> Not now to be perceived yet order's own.

Though the tone of the passage, even in its larger context, never quite defines itself, and the rhetoric is finicking and cumbersome, the lines relate directly to the passage in "The Comedian as the Letter C" in which Crispin's plan for a "poets' colony" is delineated:

> He, therefore, wrote his prolegomena,
> And, being full of the caprice, inscribed
> Commingled souvenirs and prophecies.
> He made a singular collation. Thus:
> The natives of the rain are rainy men.
> . . . .
> Upon these premises propounding, he
> Projected a colony that should extend
> To the dusk of a whistling south below the south,
> A comprehensive island hemisphere.
> The man in Georgia waking among pines
> Should be pine-spokesman. The responsive man,
> Planting his pristine cores in Florida,
> Should prick thereof, not on the psaltery,
> But on the banjo's categorical gut,
> Tuck, tuck, while the flamingoes flapped his bays. . . .

Crispin's project failed because he could not "think one thing and think it long," and because his thought followed the change of seasons and surroundings with no more than an acquiescence to "natural order," which had been his one great discovery and had destroyed him as a poet. Such a fate was easier to foresee and cope with, in some ways, than the consequences of a future in which the "natural order" has been so altered that the world no longer bears a resemblance to the one the poet knows, unless, despite such change, "ploughmen, peacocks, doves" continue to fulfill themselves in their own ways. Such an order might ultimately be one accessible to Auden's "successful artist (the one on good terms with society)," who thinks "that what is sauce for the goose is sauce for the gander," and "is an anarchist at heart who, like a

peasant proprietor, hates all government for whose inter-
ference he has no personal cause to see the necessity." And
hard as it is to think of Stevens as an anarchist or a peasant,
it is worth remembering that he said in the "Adagia," "There
must be something of the peasant in every poet." It was not
an idea, one would think, that he held tenaciously or consistently; but although he also said, somewhat ambiguously,
"Success as the result of industry is a peasant ideal," he
valued "faithful service and hard work" in his business life.
In this respect, at least, he was a characteristic American.

So long as his correspondence with Latimer flourished, and
until what he called the "little nursery turns" in Latimer's
letters began to irritate him, it provided an outlet for confidences and opinions he assumed would not be violated. The
books Latimer was publishing showed "discipline," and the
books were what mattered: *Ideas of Order* and *Owl's Clover*
would help him to circulate. He could inveigh against what
he disliked, such as "an article by Dospassos on Ford, . . .
an atrocious piece of writing and an incredible piece of thinking; and yet Dospassos is regarded as an international figure."
He unearthed "Infernale," written twenty years earlier, re-
titled it "The Guide of Alcestis," and sent it to Latimer as
"a poem which [would exist] only in [Latimer's] copy of
Ideas of Order," a private joke he must have enjoyed and a
tacit criticism of Latimer's taste. He reread many of the poems
in *Harmonium* in order to answer questions about "influences"
and "meaning." He denied any indebtedness to Valéry, and
said he had read very little of his work; and, with some
asperity, he rejected Latimer's suggestion that his poetry
had something in common with the novels of Ronald Firbank:
"To my way of thinking," he said, "there is not the slightest
bit of affectation in anything that I do. I write as I do, not
because that satisfies me, but because no other way satisfies
me. It is curious to think of the possibility that Firbank wrote
in the way he wrote, for the same reason." He recounted a
trip to New York and a visit to the Morgan Library: "Better
fifty minutes of the Morgan Library than a cycle in the Sur-

realist Exhibition. The Metaphysics of Aristotle embellished by a miniaturist who knew the meaning of the word embellishment knocks the metaphysics of Dali cold." And he sent progress reports on his new poems, which comprised *Owl's Clover.* The correspondence resolved itself into a defense of "what Mr. Filene calls 'up-to-date capitalism'" and the conviction that "one's subject is always poetry, or should be."

The labored discourse of *Owl's Clover* disappointed him almost as soon as he saw it in print, although the book as a book "set a standard." By then, he had begun to recover his poetic balance, and to think of new projects. He was asked to read on the Morris Grey Fund at Harvard—"something that I have never done before," he told Latimer, "and I look forward to it the way one must look forward to one's first baby"—where he gave his lecture on "The Irrational Element in Poetry" and read from his new book. Ben Belitt's review of the trade edition of *Ideas of Order* and *Owl's Clover* evoked a rare response, in which he said,

> The only thing wrong with the review is that it may mean more to me than to any other person. Life cancels poetry with such rapidity that it keeps one rather breathless. What I tried to do in owl's clover was to dip aspects of the contemporaneous in the poetic. You seem to think that I have produced a lot of Easter eggs, and perhaps I have.

It was the lack of aptitude for "formal discourse in the quest for order and certitude" that Belitt had criticized in the new poem, a "difficulty," Stevens asserted, of which he had long been conscious and with which he was constantly struggling. But the poem also suffered, as he himself suggested, from its contemporaneity.

Discourse was not, however, the mode he chose for his next work. Within three months he had completed most of the poems of "The Man with the Blue Guitar," which were not "abstractions" but dealt with "the painter's problem of realization: I have been trying to see the world about me

both as I see it and as it is." Whether he was forcing himself, he was not sure, but he added that his "usual experience" of allowing his subject to fill him up—to let his "thought
. . . collect in pools"—and then of expressing himself in "the
most slap-dash way" had not worked. But the variations which
formed the substance of "The Man with the Blue Guitar"
alluded to "the world as it is" so obliquely and with such
sparseness of detail that they had the quality of abstractions.
The running couplets, frequently irregular in their rhythm
and only sporadically rhymed, attempted no sustained dialogue
between the poet and those who heard his tune—the man
with the guitar and the "they" who were not so much an
audience as whoever might be within earshot of his musing.
The thick, highly elaborated rhetoric of "Owl's Clover" had
been replaced by a simpler and more obviously familiar
idiom, as deceptive in its impact as anything he ever wrote.
He was also far more interested in the world as the poet saw
it than he was in those who opposed or questioned his view
—the inhabitants of "Oxidia, banal suburb" the "unedifying
neighborhood" of Westerly Terrace, as he once called it, who
lacked imagination, or whose imagination he could not grasp.
He did not exclude himself from Oxidia, but he had too remote a knowledge of it or tolerance for it to do it justice,
much as he complained of "withering" in Hartford. He told
Hi Simons in 1940,

> About the time when I, personally, began to feel
> round for a new romanticism, I might naturally have
> been expected to start on a new cycle. Instead of
> doing so, I began to feel that I was on the edge: that
> I wanted to get to the center: that I was isolated,
> and that I wanted to share the common life. . . .
> People say that I live in a world of my own: that
> sort of thing. Instead of seeking therefore for a "re-
> lentless contact" [as Crispin had done in "The Come-
> dian as the Letter C"], I have been interested in
> what might be described as an attempt to achieve
> the normal, the central. So stated, this puts the thing

out of all proportion in respect to its relation to the
context of life. Of course, I don't agree with the people who say that I live in a world of my own; I think
that I am perfectly normal, but I see that there is
a center. For instance, a photograph of a lot of fat
men and women in the woods, drinking beer and
singing Hi-li Hi-lo convinces me that there is a normal that I ought to try to achieve.

The question he had asked in "Academic Discourse at
Havana," "Is the function of the poet here mere sound,/Sub-
tler than the ornatest prophecy,/To stuff the ear?" demanded
not so much an answer different from the one given in that
poem as one less hedged round by ambiguities and qualifi-
cations, surer in its affirmation of the essential goodness of
life, the *Drang nach den Gut* that he believed in so deeply.
It must also have occurred to him more and more often that
his failure to see "much point to the life of the ordinary man,"
which he felt distinguished him from ordinary men, like the
"center" he said he saw and somewhat arrogantly asserted
that other "normal" people did not see, posed for him an
equally complex problem. But, if he largely resisted the
"normal" which included suffering and misery, the horror of
war and injustice, it was because tragedy and suffering made
poetry personal, as his remarks on the poetry of Gene Der-
wood testify:

> . . . the pages of this book . . . contain not literary
> exercises but the text of a life: the life of a young
> woman constantly thoughtful of injustice and afraid
> and frightened of the present and of the years to
> come. I should suppose that she had read and searched
> a great deal of poetry, particularly English poetry,
> and that she had been moulded by the poetry she
> had read. In the conflict that came of all this she was
> unhappy enough not to have had the strength to pre-
> vail. She had not mastered life and I am very much
> afraid that, for that reason, she had not mastered her
> own poetry. There are many striking things in the

> book. . . . It seems to me, in the face of so much that
> moves one, that it would be wrong to speak of any
> aspects of the book other than these personal and
> human ones. After I closed the book I said to myself
> *la malheureuse.*

For all his belief that poetry has to be "a magnificent fury
or . . . nothing," one seldom finds in his poems such "personal and human" qualities, although they are, as Randall
Jarrell said, at their best "the poems of a man fully human
—of someone sympathetic, magnanimous, both brightly and
deeply intelligent . . ." And although his detachment from
"the foul rag-and-bone shop of the heart" may have denied
him access to great passion and intensity in his work, it preserved that "sane good sense" he identified with all that he
regarded as truly civilized, and of which in its own way,
his poetry became a superb example. No one, finally, was
more appreciative than he of his own good fortune.

The poet of *Ideas of Order* and *Owl's Clover* also clung
to the privilege of his own individuality as fiercely as Crispin
or Broomstick, who had remarked that for a poetess to be
"herself in her day," she "must be as free from to-day as
yesterday," or the ambitious young man who had wanted to
create a poetry of his own and a world of his own thirty-five
years earlier. In much the same way, "The Man with the Blue
Guitar" (XV) was a riposte to Grigson and a recollection of
his own doubts about some of *Harmonium's* "outmoded and
debilitated poems," as well as an "illustration" of the belief
that one should not be "modern" when there were more important things to be:

> Is this picture of Picasso's, this "hoard
> Of destructions," a picture of ourselves,
>
> Now, an image of our society?
> Do I sit, deformed, a naked egg,
>
> Catching at Good-bye, harvest moon,
> Without seeing the harvest or the moon?

> Things as they are have been destroyed.
> Have I? Am I a man that is dead
>
> At a table on which the food is cold?
> Is my thought a memory, not alive?
>
> Is the spot on the floor, there, wine or blood
> And whichever it may be, is it mine?

For Marianne Moore, it was "the interacting veins" between the early poems and the later ones which provided
the greatest and most continuing source of satisfaction; and
there is little doubt that the period between 1935 and 1941
was one of reexamination and reevaluation. From this point
of view, "Owl's Clover" and "The Man with the Blue Guitar" were pivotal poems. He revised and "tightened up"
"Owl's Clover"; but even the version printed in *The Man
with the Blue Guitar and Other Poems* failed to satisfy him
when he came to put together the *Collected Poems,* and he
omitted it and two other "rhetorical" pieces, "The Woman
That Had More Babies Than That" and "Life on a Battle-
ship," neither of which mastered the art of discourse more
successfully than "Owl's Clover." But the theme of "The
Man with the Blue Guitar," wittily and arrestingly varied
but never really resolved, had opened up a new subject, the
end of which he had hardly "got to," as he told Latimer;
and the poems of *Parts of a World* bore him out.

He had, furthermore, to settle some of the conflict within
himself: the contradiction, for example, implicit in his statement that his critics did not see the kind of world in which
he was living and his equally strong conviction that he was
simply a contemporary man who happened to write poetry.
He knew that "it is not every day that the world arranges
itself in a poem," but he could not wait upon inspiration; and
because he continued to think that he was, of necessity, a
weekend poet for whom writing took the place of holidays
as well, he never thought of himself as a prolific writer like
William Carlos Williams who, he said, "wrote a little every

day and always had a house full of manuscripts." And as his
own concern for "what a writer has to say" became more
acute, it seemed to him that Williams was "more interested
in the way of saying things than in what he [had] to say":
he told Barbara Church in 1953, that the paintings of Nicolas
de Staël, which "could well become fashionable" but "would
mean nothing at all" to him, answered "one question" he
would "state in terms of poetry: if the present generation
[liked] the mobile-like arrangement of lines to be found in
the work of William Carlos Williams or the verbal con-
glomerates of e. e. cummings," what would the next generation like? "Pretty much the bare page, for that alone
would be new, the way de Staël likes the bare canvas." In
the meantime, "the painter's problem of realization" provided
the impetus for a whole series of poems.

His interest in painting and painters had kept pace with
his interest in music and poetry, and his library included a
large collection of exhibition catalogs which gave him, if
they were "well written," as much satisfaction as he got
"from most poetry." In addition, he had begun to acquire
a few paintings from Anatole Vidal, his bookseller in Paris:
a Brianchon, a Cavaillès, a Brayer, a Marchand, a Ceria, a
de la Patellière, a Henri Lebasque, a Marthe Lebasque, and
a portrait of Vidal himself by Jean Labasque, all minor and
latter-day examples of the Impressionist tradition, which remained for him the great thing in art. His first interest in
collecting, years earlier, when he had known Carl Zigrosser
at the Weyhe Gallery in New York, had centered on the
prints and etchings of Marius Bauer, Daumier, Goya, Jong-
kind, Legros, Lepere, Meryon, Millet, Rembrandt, and Childe
Hassam. But he had collected very little then. He owned a
Pissarro drawing, a Braque lithograph, two Hiroshige prints,
some etchings by Ian Strang and Francis Dodd, a lithograph
by Rodin. He had no illusions about becoming a great col-
lector or a proud possessor; but that he left the choice of his
paintings to someone else when he reached the point at
which he could collect in a small way was curious.

It was not simply that someone in Paris could purchase paintings for him more cheaply than he could have purchased them in a New York gallery. He admitted that the descriptions of some of the pictures he received were better than the pictures themselves, but he was willing to risk the disappointment. "I am one of the many people," he once wrote, "who live from time to time in a Paris that has never existed and that is composed of the things that other people, primarily Parisians themselves, have said about Paris. That particular Paris communicates an interest in life that may be wholly fiction, but if so, it is precious fiction." "If I should ever go to Paris," he once said, "the first person I should meet there would probably be myself. I have been there so often." Paintings from Paris, like tea and jaggary from Ceylon, gave concreteness to his fiction and kept intact the element of spontaneity and surprise which preserved him from routine. They were a source of renewal, not "prodigious specimens," but things "natural to him, or he to them," "une fenêtre fleurie," "things light and not dark, cheerful and not gloomy, and . . . above everything else . . . something real but saturated with the feeling and the imagination of the artist." Braque, Matisse, Klee—these were three "modern" painters he greatly liked; Matisse and Klee because of their gaiety and lightness, Braque in spite of what he called his "modern perversions":

> There is a siccity and an ascetic quality about his color that is very much to my liking. Some of his greens and browns are almost disciplinary. In his case, his modern perversions are not particularly offensive. On the other hand, I find such things particularly offensive in the work of younger men of little or no intelligence. After all, one can be as much ravished by severity as by indulgence.

But he had "a taste for Braque and a purse for Bombois," by his own admission, and like most other people seeking support for their own point of view, sometimes invented the evidence to sustain it. He would have enjoyed being the discoverer of a new artist of the rectitude, as he called it, that reflected his own devotion to poetry; but it is likely that he would have enjoyed keeping the knowledge of the discovery to himself. At the same time, he confessed that he did not have the courage to purchase a painting by an artist of whom he had never heard, and after World War II he devoted considerable energy to making himself knowledgeable about young and promising Paris painters.

As always, the paintings he did acquire contributed to his poems: Marchand's "Les Oliviers" to "Connoisseur of Chaos," a Tal Coat still life to "Angel Surrounded by Paysans." Sure as he was, however, of his own preferences in art, he found it difficult to say, "This is my taste, it may not be another man's," without self-defensiveness. It was not until he was asked to write an appreciation of Marcel Gromaire for an exhibition catalog in 1949, which he carried out very much in the French manner, and "Raoul Dufy: A Note," intended as an introduction to the lithographs of *La Fée Electricité* in 1953, that he was able to master his own bias with success. The lecture, "The Relations between Poetry and Painting," which he delivered at the Museum of Modern Art in 1951, belonged, as he himself knew, to his fragmentary "theory of poetry," and had grown out of his belief that "to a large extent, the problems of poets are the problems of painters, and poets must often turn to the literature of painting for a discussion of their own problems."

So early a poem as "Cy Est Pourtraicte, Madame Ste Ursule, et Les Unze Milles Vierges" foreshadowed this interest in the relation of poetry to painting; it was as much a commentary on the way the illustrator of St. Ursula's story had seen her as it was an irreverently witty and modern interpretation of sainthood. And as Michel Benamou has pointed out in his essay, "Wallace Stevens: Some Relations between Poetry and Painting," the "pictorial method of composition," his "gifts as a colorist," the "paraphernalia of Cubism," and most of all, the "impulse toward transparence, his desire to be 'at the center of a diamond,' his obsession with . . . the *fraicheur* of sight, bespeak the Impressionist's dream of a translucent vision, free from memory and artifice." Benamou quotes from a letter to Mlle. Vidal, who bought pictures for Stevens after the death of her father: "I share your pleasure in the Impressionistic school. In the pictures of this school: so light in tone, so bright in color, one is not conscious of the medium. The pictures are like nature. . . ."

Moreover, as the threat to his well-being, which had momentarily shaken him during the early days of the Depression, became more remote, his interest in these aesthetic relationships reasserted itself. The air was not so heavily charged with the "anxieties and tensions" that had made it impossible, when he dropped into a gallery, to be interested in what he saw there. "The general feeling at the office," he told James A. Powers in 1937, was 'high and optimistic. . . . One feels that the wheels are going round more neatly, which is, after all, an immense thing in a world in which most of the wheels are scraping and squalling."

It is not surprising, therefore, that many of the poems following "The Man with the Blue Guitar" should be preoccupied with the difference between "What in nature merely grows" and its composition "in the way you speak/You arrange, the thing," between the thing itself and the way it is seen. In "Add This to Rhetoric," "the sense creates the pose." In "Study of Two Pears,"

> The pears are not viols,
> Nudes or bottles.
> They resemble nothing else.
> . . . .
> The pears are not seen
> As the observer wills.

In "The Poems of Our Climate," "a world of clear water, brilliant-edged," of "clear water in a brilliant bowl,/Pink and white carnations," is not enough:

There would still remain the never-resting mind,
So that one would want to escape, come back
To what had been so long composed.
The imperfect is our paradise.
Note that, in this bitterness, delight,
Since the imperfect is so hot in us,
Lies in flawed words and stubborn sounds.

In "The Latest Freed Man," "it was how the sun came shining into his room: . . . It was everything bulging and blazing
and big in itself,/The blue of the rug, the portrait of Vidal,/
Qui fait fi des joliesses banales, the chairs." In "Connoisseur
of Chaos," it was the discovery that "a law of inherent op-
posites,/Of essential unity, is as pleasant as port,/As pleasant
as the brush-strokes of a bough,/An upper, particular bough
in, say, Marchand." And in "The Common Life," the "black
line beside a white line," the light which reduces a man to
"a result/A demonstration," and leaves a woman "without
rose and without violet," suggest those abstractions in which
the imagination of the artist reveals the impoverished imagination of contemporary life. The poem comes to the same
conclusion as "Disillusionment of Ten O'Clock," but the
gaiety of the earlier poem is to the discursiveness of the later
poem almost as the vividness of one of Les Fauves is to the
dryness of an abstract expressionist.

He was also casting about for ways of clarifying other convictions, of giving his life as a poet something of "a straight
course" and freeing it from the "mass of irrelevancies" that
had brought about Crispin's downfall. He knew better than
anyone else the need for a stock-taking by the time he had
finished "The Man with the Blue Guitar." His correspondence
with Latimer involved him in a good many questions he had
never before been asked, some of which he fended off with
considerable grace, some of which he tried to answer as
explicitly as he could, but with a growing realization that he
had taken the validity of some of his ideas too much for
granted, even to himself. He had also made assumptions about

the relation of his more recent work to his earlier work which
required examination. When Latimer proposed a "collected
poems" early in 1938, Stevens liked the idea, particularly
"of 100 copies only, for sale, and not too many presentation
copies," and added: "At the moment the status of the book
deluxe is disintegrating about as rapidly as other things deluxe." He thought that "The Comedian as the Letter C"
had "gathered a good deal of dust," and might be eliminated;
but he also said that he thought he knew what he wanted to
do next and that it would take a long time, "without an opportunity to do anything else."

Latimer disappeared into the Orient shortly afterward.
Meanwhile, Hi Simons, a Chicago publisher who was preparing a bibliography of Stevens's work, had asked for assistance
in tracking down early and uncollected material. Impressed
by Simons's knowledge, he generously sent him whatever
he had. The affinity Simons felt for the poetry became clear
a year or so later, when his article on "The Comedian as the
Letter C" was published in the *Southern Review;* and the
exchange of letters that followed provides the most nearly
complete and exhaustive series of commentaries on the poems
that we have. The tact with which Simons waited until proving himself as an explicator before asking further questions
made it easier for him to draw Stevens out. Simons concluded
his essay with a question: "What happens, through fifteen
years of accelerating social disintegration, to a poet who iden-
tifies himself with things as they are?" Because the question
was of great import to Stevens himself, and was in itself evidence that Simons took him seriously, he was willing to forego
his decision not to explain his work. Besides, as he said in an
earlier letter to Simons, ". . . what one is after in all these
things is the discovery of a value that really suffices":

> The ordinary, everyday search of the romantic mind
> is rewarded perhaps rather too lightly by the satis-
> faction that it finds in what it calls reality. But if one
> happened to be playing checkers somewhere under
> the Maginot Line, subject to a call at any moment

to do some job that might be one's last job, one
would spend a good deal of time thinking in order
to make the situation seem reasonable, inevitable
and free from question.

I suppose that, in the last analysis, my own main
óbjective is to do that kind of thinking. On the other
hand, [a poem like "Variations on a Summer Day,"]
. . . from which every bit of anything of that sort has
been excluded, also has its justifications. In a world
permanently enigmatical, to hear and see agreeable
things involves something more than mere imagism.
One might do it deliberately and in this particular
poem I did it deliberately.

Simons was most interested in "Owl's Clover" and "The
Man with the Blue Guitar," and during 1940, Stevens "saturated" himself in both poems, in order to answer the numerous questions Simons had asked. Occasionally he provided
paraphrases; much of what he did was to give a key to his
idiom: thus, "to chop the sullen psaltery" equalled "to write
poetry with difficulty, because of excess of realism of life";
and in the line, "time grows upon the rock," "time = life,
and the rock = the world." His comments would have been
better "in conversation," where they would not have become
so "fixed"; written down, they tended to reduce the poems
to elaborate allegories. On the other hand, the incidental
observations with which the explanations were laced revealed
how rapidly he was moving away in 1940 from the kind of
poem he had written in "Variations on a Summer Day"—
the poem dedicated to the "casual" aspects of earth, "light
or color, images"—toward the poem which, in his own words,
would be "of the mind in the act of finding/What will suffice,"
a poem of synthesis in which "cross-reflections, modifications,
counter-balances, complements, giving and taking are illimitable," and of which he insisted "The Old Woman and the
Statue" was "a perfect illustration," and "The Statue at the
World's End" was "a still better one." He was trying hard
to rescue "Owl's Clover" for the canon, hoping perhaps that
an explication by Simons would help; but he also admitted

that "The Greenest Continent" (Part III of "Owl's Clover")
seemed "to be a bit of *reportage*, and it [did] in fact look
superficial regarded as to its actual text." He valued "A Duck
for Dinner" because "the artist, that is to say, the man of
imagination," was there proposed as "the ethereal compound-
er, pater patriae, the patriarch wearing the diamond crown
of crowns, that is: the crown of life . . ." He valued "Sombre
Figuration" because

> The truth is that, when the imagination no longer
> partakes to the degree that it should of the real, we
> reject it and restore ourselves in the hum-drum. And
> in hum-drum space, when the imagination has ended,
> we feel the rapture of a time, etc. We want a reality,
> we want to be, to enjoy being, etc. Reaction. (End)!

Quite clearly "Owl's Clover" represented to him an embodiment of his own desires for poetry and the poet and was in
its way an "illustration" of the "cross-reflections . . . [and the
illimitable] giving and taking" that defined his own life as a
man and as a poet. It was another step toward the realization
of his unyielding determination "to live in the world but
outside of existing conceptions of it," to be the poet who
was the man who "feels *abundantly* the poetry of everything,"
who has "something by nature and [knows] more about the
world by reason thereof," who wins acceptance on his own
terms, and who, for all his uniqueness, is a contemporary man
who happens to write poetry—the poet, once again, of "Academic Discourse at Havana":

> As part of nature he is part of us.
> His rarities are ours: may they be fit
> And reconcile us to our selves in those
> True reconcilings, dark, pacific words . . .

The figure of such a possible poet began to appear in the
poems roughly contemporary with the long letters to Simons,
in the "sleight-of-hand man," "The Well Dressed Man with
a Beard," the hero, the "man of glass,/Who in a million dia-

monds sums us up," the "anti-master man, floribund ascetic,"
the lecturer giving "Addresses to the Academy of Fine Ideas,"
the "prisoner" of "Montrachet-le-Jardin," or "the mind"
itself, especially in a time of war, for, as he says in "Man
and Bottle":

> The mind is the great poem of winter, the man,
> Who, to find what will suffice,
> Destroys romantic tenements
> Of rose and ice
>
> In a land of war. More than the man, it is
> A man with the fury of a race of men,
> A light at the centre of many lights,
> A man at the centre of men.
>
> It has to content the reason concerning war,
> It has to persuade that war is part of itself,
> A manner of thinking, a mode
> Of destroying, as the mind destroys,
>
> An aversion, as the world is averted
> From an old delusion, an old affair with the sun,
> An impossible aberration with the moon,   ·
> A grossness of peace.
>
> It is not the snow that is the quill, the page.
> The poem lashes more fiercely than the wind,
> As the mind, to find what will suffice, destroys
> Romantic tenements of rose and ice.

In the world of 1940, Stevens would perhaps have said, as
he did say of the world of 1936, it was "impossible to project
a world that [would] not appear to some a deformation";
and since "the man, the poet, by synecdoche becomes poetry,"
no single characterization of him could truly "suffice." Yet
the effort had to be made, not only because "it is the ex-

planations of things that we make to ourselves that disclose
our character," but also because, "if the mind is the most
terrible force in the world, it is also the only force that de-
fends us against terror." The reexamination of *Ideas of Order,*
"Owl's Clover," and "The Man with the Blue Guitar" led
not only to a clarification of thought but also to "new explanations of things," new subjects for new poems, which were
additional symbols of himself or his various selves; and they
laid the foundation for "Notes toward a Supreme Fiction,"
and for the theory of poetry which he was already discussing
with Henry Church.

Stevens's friendship with Church was, beyond all question,
the great friendship of his life as a poet, and perhaps the
greatest he ever knew as a man. Early in 1942, when he had
not heard from Church in some months, and was worried that
he might have "offended" him, Stevens wrote in answer to
a welcome letter:

> I love to hear from you. You have so thoroughly
> lived the life that I should have been glad to live,
> and you are so much more intricate a personality
> than any half dozen people that I can think of put
> together, that I felt that I had lost a good deal more
> than one would ordinarily lose as the result of a
> difficulty.

The life Church had lived before returning to America because of World War II had been that of the artist-patron free
to follow his own interests as he wished. Heir to an indus-
trial fortune, and a member of the board of directors of the
firm his family had established (Church and Dwight), he was
rich enough to live in Europe, in the world of arts and letters,
for forty years of his life. He was the founder and coeditor
with Jean Paulhan of *Mesures;* and it was a request for a
selection of poems from *Harmonium,* to be published in translation in an American number of the magazine, which had
begun the correspondence. Stevens took the initiative—al-

though he did not plan "to develop into a large-sized correspondent"—partly because he was interested to learn that
Church was an American whose mother had been born in
Hartford, partly because of his own interest in the translations of his poems, and, it seems likely, partly because Church's
dedication to France and things French spoke directly to an
aspect of his own character. Asked about his intentions as a
poet, he replied:

> What counts, I suppose, is one's relations to con-
> temporary ideas. Much of that, however, would be
> irrelevant to a group of poems obviously having noth-
> ing to do with the ideas of the day in which they
> were written, nor of today. I am, in the long run,
> interested in pure poetry. No doubt from the Marxian
> point of view this sort of thing is incredible, but pure
> poetry is rather older and tougher than Marx and
> will remain so. My own way out toward the future
> involves a confidence in the spiritual role of the poet,
> who will somehow have to assist the painter, etc.
> (any artist, to tell the truth) in restoring to the imagi-
> nation what it is losing at such a catastrophic pace,
> and in supporting what it has gained.

He did not have to say to Church, as he felt he had to say
to Simons, "Poetry is a passion, not a habit." Church was one
of the "anointed."

They met for the first time late in 1939; and as their friendship grew, Church asked him for suggestions about the possibility of publishing *Mesures* in America once the war made its
continuance in France impossible. With a deference matched
only by his realization that Church had given him the opportunity to think as widely and expansively—as unsystematically
and as deeply—as he wanted to about the things closest to
him, Stevens replied not only in detail but with a sense of
excitement; and when Church proposed the establishment
of a foundation at Princeton, he countered with an additional
proposal, "the Henry Church Chair of Poetry at Harvard:

that is to say, a chair for the study of poetic thought and of
the theory of poetry." He felt that "educators would sniff
at such a thing, since it seems to be considered that univer-
sities do the Arts and Letters more harm than good," but
he also thought that "such a chair with, say, Jean Paulhan
as its first incumbent might turn the tables on the educators."
Although nothing finally came of the "Memorandum" he drew
up for Church—not even "a thrilling winter trying to give
outline and form to a thing certainly as much entitled to it
as philosophy"—it undoubtedly played its part in Church's
decision to establish the "*Mesures* Lectures" at Princeton,
and it led directly to "The Noble Rider and the Sound of
Words," which Stevens delivered at the first of the series in
1941. Even more important was the impetus that such thinking
about "the poetic side of life . . . the abstraction and the
theory" provided for "Notes toward a Supreme Fiction,"
which he began early in February 1942, immediately after
sending the manuscript of *Parts of a World* off to Knopf,
and completed by the first of June. He asked Church if he
might dedicate this "small series of poems" to him: "by way
of showing appreciation of your kindness to me last spring,
and generally, just because I should like to . . ." Except for
"Like Decorations in a Nigger Cemetery," it was the only
work he ever specifically dedicated to a friend.

Intermittent as the correspondence was, it spanned more
topics and revealed more of the man than any other group of
letters that has survived. He could write to Church of personal
things: the death of his sister, the last member of his family;
his interest in genealogy; his uncertainty about stepping into
the "academic world" and his need for "support" at such
gatherings as the Princeton lectures and *Les Entretiens de
Pontigny* at Mount Holyoke, where he read "The Figure of
the Youth as Virile Poet," the companion piece to "The Noble
Rider." He could handle a practical matter, such as Church's
request for advice in drawing up a will, with the skill and
sure knowledge of the kind of lawyer Church needed. But when
his daughter "disappointed" him by leaving Vassar, he re-

marked only that "one of the advantages of not having children is that you avoid these extraordinary complications of
character," and went on to say, "I am glad that we can go
back to the subject of a Chair of Poetry." His frankness about
his contemporaries in the world of letters revealed both the
austerity of his judgments and an ability to give his own intolerances the quality of obiter dicta, as if, at times, what he
regarded as "unprincipled thinking" were the measure of a
man's humanity. "Life is not people and scene," he noted in
the "Adagia," "but thought and feeling." He lived in his mind;
and since it was true for him that "the more intensely one
feels something that one likes the more one is willing for it
to be what it is," the more intensely he disliked a thing, the
more he felt justified in discounting its significance, not only
for himself, but for others. Yet he seldom carried his "prin-
cipled thinking" to extremes. Nothing, in the long run, cost
him more effort than learning to tolerate and accept those
views of experience which violated his own—not in art or
politics or even philosophy, so much as in his belief that
egotism lay at the bottom of human experience and values.

Yet it puzzled him, as he told Church, that "in not a single
review of PARTS OF A WORLD was there even so much as
a suggestion that the book gave the man who read it any
pleasure." He was, however, gratified that *Notes toward a
Supreme Fiction* had pleased Jean Wahl, for "to give pleasure
to an intelligent man . . . is as much as one can expect." Even
Hi Simons, who had written "an exceedingly intelligent notice"
of *Parts of a World*, had not expressed pleasure in the book,
although his review was the only one that Stevens could think
of as "helping one to be accepted . . . the sort of thing that
is meant when you ask for a book by so-and-so." He knew, of
course, that *Notes toward a Supreme Fiction* was a far more
significant book than *Parts of a World;* and despite his fear
that it would be "blanketed" by the larger volume, he was
himself pleased to find the response to it much greater and
more in keeping with his own hopes for it than he had expected it to be.

If thinking about "the reality of the war" interfered with his writing for a time, he still had his correspondence and his genealogical research, and more and more reading to occupy him. His correspondence with Hi Simons picked up, now concerned with *Notes toward a Supreme Fiction* and with *Harmonium*, and was cut short only by the death of Simons in 1945; indeed, although he felt he must refuse to read Simons's study, "Wallace Stevens and Mallarmé," which had been submitted to the Cummington Press, their exchange of letters suffered no real break. The first edition of *Notes toward a Supreme Fiction* (270 copies) sold out within six months of publication; a second edition (330 copies), published in November 1943, did almost as well. There were the beginnings of new correspondences and the renewals of old friendships, some from the distant past. He sidestepped involvement in the controversy over his poetry between Yvor Winters and Theodore Weiss. He wrote "Esthétique du Mal" for the *Kenyon Review* in something less than six weeks, on a subject suggested by a letter John Crowe Ransom had quoted in his article, "Artists, Soldiers, Positivists": "the relation between poetry and what [the author of the letter] called pain." Nicholas Moore, of The Fortune Press in London, wrote to make arrangements for a selected volume; a project that ultimately concluded with an unauthorized *Selected Poems* in 1952, a few weeks before the authorized edition was published by Faber and Faber, and a contretemps which resulted in the destruction of all but a handful of copies of the Fortune Press book, making it thus the rarest of all his volumes. In January 1945, a correspondence began with José Rodriguez Feo, a young graduate of Harvard from Cuba, which lasted until Stevens's death, and was, like the correspondence with Church, a source of continuing delight—and in three or four instances, a source of poems. His correspondence with Leonard van Geyzel, who had done some "shopping" for him in Ceylon before the war, began again in 1945, as did the even more satisfying one with Paule Vidal, the daughter of his Paris bookseller. The Cummington Press published *Esthétique du*

Mal in an edition as elegant and fastidious as the text itself, with hand-colored illustrations by Wightman Williams. Harvard invited him to compose and read the Phi Beta Kappa poem, the subject of which became his title, "Description without Place," and as he told Church:

> It seems to me to be an interesting idea: that is to say, the idea that we live in the description of a place and not in the place itself, and in every vital sense we do. This ought to be a good subject for such an occasion. I suppose there is nothing more helpful to a poem than to have someone to read it to, and that particular audience ought to be a good audience.

He was elected to the National Institute of Arts and Letters in 1945. He refused with all the prudence and detachment one would expect, to take part in "The Case for and against Ezra Pound," which Charles Norman compiled and edited for *PM*. "While [Pound] may have many excuses," he wrote in a letter that was not to be used in any way, "I must say that I don't consider the fact that he is a man of genius as an excuse. Surely such men are subject to the common disciplines." He thought the real question was one of Pound's motive, and suggested that any controversy be delayed until Norman knew why Pound "did what he did before rallying to his defense."

Throughout this whole period, the acceptance he had come to think of such importance manifested itself in the awards and honors that he never thought relevant to his interest in poetry, but which, as they accumulated, tempered his impatience with those whose interests and values were alien if not inimical to his own. His letters spoke more and more often of the "pressure of reality" which threatened to crush the imagination, and of the misery of Europe which seemed to him more real in March 1946 than it had six months earlier. Reading a group of his own poems in *Origenes*, the magazine José Rodriguez Feo had founded in Havana, he said of them that "after the lapse of six months or more from the time when they were written," they seemed "academic and unreal":

One is inclined, therefore, to sympathize with one's more unsympathetic critics. It is all well enough to say that, in the long run, what was appropriate once will be appropriate again, but it does not follow; after all, nothing follows. The life of a poet, like the life of a painter, is just as difficult and unpredictable as the life of a speculator in Wall Street. But if a poet experiences these eras in which what he thinks and writes seems to be otiose, he is bound to recognize that, in the same eras, almost everything that other people write, as well as the pictures they paint, and the music they write seems to be equally otiose. Yet to live exclusively in reality is as intolerable as it is incomprehensible, and I can say this even though yesterday, after playing a little Debussy on the gramophone, I thought how exactly he sounded like Chaminade.

The poems which had followed *Notes toward a Supreme Fiction* had tried, as he said in answer to the question of what he considered the greatest problem facing the young writer in America in 1946, to absorb "the general life: the public life." The politician, and not the philosopher, was the enemy of poetry, and since poetry was on the side of freedom and individuality, the poet's role had to be more than a private role:

If people are to become dependent on poetry for any of the fundamental satisfactions, poetry must have an increasingly intellectual scope and power. This is a time for the highest poetry. We never understood the world less than we do now nor, as we understand it, liked it less. We never wanted to understand it more or needed to like it more. These are the intense compulsions that challenge the poet as the appreciatory creator of values and beliefs. That, finally, states the problem.

The statement of the problem, as always, was easier than the

solution—even though he said in the "Adagia," "It is necessary to propose an enigma to the mind. The mind always
proposes a solution." Yet nowhere was there evidence that
he had abandoned the belief, as he put in a letter to his Harvard classmate, Gilbert Montague, "that it might be possible
for us to believe in something that we know to be untrue."
"Of course," he added, "we do that every day, but we don't
make the most of the fact that we do it out of the need to
believe, what in your day, and mine, in Cambridge was called
the will to believe."

He had said much the same thing to Church:

> There are things with respect to which we willingly
> suspend disbelief; if there is instinctive in us a will
> to believe, or if there is a will to believe, whether
> or not it is instinctive, it seems to me that we can
> suspend disbelief with reference to a fiction as easily
> as we can suspend it with reference to anything else.
> There are fictions that are extensions of reality. There
> are plenty of people who believe in Heaven as defi-
> nitely as your New England ancestors and my Dutch
> ancestors believed in it. But Heaven is an extension
> of reality.

So, too, in discussing the exact nature of his supreme fiction
with Simons, he had at first not wanted to identify it as poetry,
although he said that his next task would be "to try to be a
little more precise about this enigma." Yet he held off, because "as soon as I start to rationalize, I lose the poetry
of the idea." Poetry had been the supreme fiction to begin
with; and the supreme fiction would be poetry again—for
nothing meant more to him than poetry. When he sent the
manuscript of *Transport to Summer* to Knopf in 1947, he
placed "Notes toward a Supreme Fiction" at the end, although it was the earliest poem in the manuscript, and had
been followed by such ambitious essays in the poetry of reality
as "Esthétique du Mal" and "Credences of Summer." It remained the culmination of his thought, of the life of his mind.

THE LATER POEMS

THE PURE POETRY of *Harmonium* insofar as it relates to the later poetry is not limited to the "casual" aspects of earth, "light or color, images," nor to the "poetry of words" and the "gaiety of language." But these qualities dominate the book and give it its special, even unique character. Of the poems in which light and color play the most important role, "Sea Surface Full of Clouds" is the most brilliant. The cumulative effect of its repetitions and rhythms, and its beautifully controlled rhymes, although they may be no more than "mechanisms," as Stevens told John Pauker, does produce a detachment in the reader: one becomes entranced with the play of water and cloud, the "resemblances" between them, in such a way that the poem becomes momentarily at least "a revelation of nature." As the moving light in each of the five cantos touches the desk of the ship to illumine sea and sky in a repetition that is more than a repetition and never the same twice—diffusing, massing, unfolding, loosening, tossing—playing upon the constantly changing and ever-present clouds and water, the mind is touched to a kind of wakefulness and responsiveness. Who, then, the mind asks, catches this superb panorama, the "strange relations" it evokes of colors and chocolate and umbrellas? Who gives the "machine" of ocean its meaning? Not, Stevens seems to imply, the "soul" or the ego; and although imagination might very well designate the

force or spirit he means, imagination is too abstract a word
to describe so powerful, mysterious, and pervasive a force.
It cannot easily be denominated in language, because in his
most profound experience of its power, it evades definition.
And so he uses French, varying the phrases to describe its
effect on each of the five mornings, the sound of which is as
essential to its "meaning" as any literal English equivalent—
indeed, any translation impoverishes the poem by robbing it
of part of its mystery. So it is that the imagination transforms
the world, "refreshes life" and reality, and allows one to see
ocean and sky as "the veritable thing" in all their glistening,
crystalline clarity.

Beyond this it was impossible to go in this direction, although he wrote other poems with the same intention off
and on for the rest of his life: "The Dwarf," "Of Hartford in
a Purple Light," "Variations on a Summer Day," "The News
and the Weather," the "Six Discordant Songs" ("Metamorphosis" and the five poems that follow it), and "Things of
August"; but only once or twice, in "Some Friends from
Pascagoula" and "Autumn Refrain," with the same breath-
taking skill and success. An alternative suggested itself in the
poems which sought to define the relationship between "what
we see" and "what we think," and in the poems delineating
the mind's struggle to discover "what will suffice" to make
life "complete in itself," an effort which provided its own
satisfactions and all the drama he required. In one of the
least pretentious but most perceptive essays on Stevens, Louis
Martz has called attention to Stevens's "admiration for the
power of thinking, for the constructive power of deliberate
choice," which meant perception and perceiving even more
than feeling or conception and conceptualizing, but always,
in the finest poems, a single activity involving all three: in
the final analysis, what has always been meant by "making."
This unified activity is evident in many of the "anecdotal"
poems of Harmonium, but the oddness of its results was per-
plexing, compared with most Imagist poetry and much of the
traditional verse of the time, or with the poetry which found

its raw material in the city, or small town life, machinery and technology, and the political and artistic ideologies competing for the allegiance of the reader as well as of the poet. In a time when *mere* oddness was often confused with originality, it was not implausible for *Harmonium* to be admired for qualities Stevens neither aimed at nor valued. The vocabulary which Marianne Moore has characterized as "benign," the fastidiousness and delight in elegance and color, and the pre-occupation with "the right sensation," lent themselves to an easy identification with hedonism and dandyism; the concern with the self made it easy to think of the poetry as private and against the democratic grain. Such qualities do appear in his work; and readers who have found them unacceptable cannot be regarded as altogether insensitive to its virtues, or vulgarly wrong-headed. On the other hand, the attempts of a good many of his recent critics to see the poetry as the embodiment or statement of a self-contained philosophic order in which the poems themselves are of little intrinsic interest, represent an even more gross misunderstanding of his achieve-ment—and, one can say, of poetry itself. Yet here, too, the very fabric of the verse can tempt one into such an error. That the voice in which the poem speaks is seldom the voice of a character whom one can recognize, or with whom one can readily identify—a Bottom or a Prospero, a Prufrock or an Eben Flood, or even a Ulysses as Tennyson saw him—is one source of difficulty. The self that speaks in his poems, although sure of its identity, uses a language that is both un-mistakable and unfamiliar; and sometimes the poetry is so much a poetry of things that do not exist without the words which give them being, that it seems to lack a recognizable human voice at all. Yet these "things" do not really exist in a vacuum: more often than not, they belong to the world of commonplace reality, but they are viewed from an odd angle and in a light that makes them look unfamiliar, as in the paintings of Paul Klee. Nature dominates his world: sun, moon, stars, flowers, birds, "the junipers shagged with ice," "a Schuyl-kill in mid-earth," "the large-leaved day," Vesuvius, the "dust

that traverses a shade"; but it also contains a good many of
man's artifacts: "socks of lace/And beaded ceintures," tin cans
and lard pails, "the down-town frieze," "Marianna's cart,"
"the window that makes it difficult/To say good-by to the
past," statuary and music; and, at the beginning and the end of
his life as a poet, the woman of "Sunday Morning," the "you"
of "Peter Quince at the Clavier" and the "we" of "Le Monocle de Mon Oncle," the "old philosopher," "a man/Come
back to see a certain house," and the aged Ariel of "The
Planet on the Table." Even in the poems in which no speaker
or thinker is identified, or in which he exists as some otherwise anonymous "one," it is usually possible to catch a glimpse
of "the artist, the presence of the determining personality,"
the "reality" without which "no amount of other things matters much."

"Academic Discourse at Havana" had put the question of
the "function" of the poet to the maker who had exhausted
the possibilities of a world in which order seemed fixed and
unchanging, even before the final apotheosis of that world
had been realized in "Sea Surface Full of Clouds." Although
its answer suggested that the self comprised several selves,
which the poet had to "reconcile" to each other in "dark,
pacific words," and to nature, of which he and they were all
"a part," the order of the world had altered by the time
Stevens returned to poetry. The "world in flux" which had
sustained him still followed its cyclic changes of season, but
Miami had become a "jamboree of hoodlums" and Key West
had grown "literary." This was a change he had foreseen,
but it still had to be reckoned with. "Academic Discourse at
Havana," although it strove to compose a "benediction,
sepulcher,/And epitaph" for the world of *Harmonium,* had
ended with the possibility that the poet's speech might be
no more than

> An incantation that the moon defines
> By mere example, opulently clear.

Life itself, "an old casino in a wood," might do no more than "define"

> An infinite incantation of our selves
> In the grand decadence of the perished swans

which were the symbol of the vanished flights of his imagination.

As early as 1926, he told Harriet Monroe,

> Perhaps, when the boom is over . . . something of [Miami's] colonial period of five or ten years ago will re-emerge and it will be possible to be at one's ease again. The little town of Everglades is as yet unaffected by the excitement, although the railroad from Fort Myers is slowly creeping downward. It may be, after all, that in a few years the only true temples will have to be found in Tobago or in the mountains of Venezuela.

He returned to Florida so long as it provided a retreat for the mind; but most of the Florida poems in *Ideas of Order* reflected unease, not the "mere being" he had once enjoyed there. The most famous of them, "The Idea of Order at Key West," echoes the beautiful lines of "Academic Discourse at Havana":

> How pale and how possessed a night it is,
> How full of exhalations of the sea . . .

in its own conclusion, but in an exhortation that modifies and deepens the tone; for in the later poem, it is the "maker's" "rage for order" which asserts itself with such urgency, rather than the comic resignation of "the grand decadence of the perished swans":

> Ramon Fernandez, tell me, if you know,
> Why, when the singing ended and we turned

> Toward the town, tell why the glassy lights,
> The lights in the fishing boats at anchor there,
> As the night descended, tilting in the air,
> Mastered the night and portioned out the sea,
> Fixing emblazoned zones and fiery poles,
> Arranging, deepening, enchanting night.
>
> Oh! Blessed rage for order, pale Ramon,
> The maker's rage to order words of the sea,
> Words of the fragrant portals, dimly-starred,
> And of ourselves and of our origins,
> In ghostlier demarcations, keener sounds.

The exhortation of "Some Friends from Pascagoula" (not Florida, but still the "far South" that he loved) moves with astonishing vitality; and the quick, controlled energy of the rhymes is unlike anything else in the book—or in the whole body of the poetry, although it is almost a complement to "Ploughing on Sunday." So, too, the witty self-scrutiny of "Sailing after Lunch" seems to be sustained by its unexpected and unexceptionable formality. But it was no accident, when the trade edition of *Ideas of Order* was issued, that "Farewell to Florida," begun before he left Pirate's Cove in 1936, stood at the beginning of the book. So placed, it redefined the tone of all that followed, pointing up the change of scene, the change of season, the new sense of the poet's relation to himself and his world. And as our own perspective on these "Northern" and often autumnal poems lengthens, the more poignant, the more personal and moving they become, although that was hardly their intention. Though many of them lack the certitude and finesse of the best poems of *Harmonium*, they define very well the sense of what it meant to be a poet in a difficult time for poetry, much as *Responsibilities* defined in 1914 a similar sense, albeit more directly and with greater emotion, for Yeats. The blemishes of indulgence in mannerism, the strain of pumping up floods of color, only faintly disfigure "A Postcard from the Volcano," "Evening without

Angels," "Lions in Sweden," and "Anglais Mort à Florence";
and they disappear entirely in "The Brave Man" and "Autumn
Refrain," which was written no later than 1931:

> The skreak and skritter of evening gone
> And grackles gone and sorrows of the sun,
> The sorrows of sun, too, gone . . . the moon and moon,
> The yellow moon of words about the nightingale
> In measureless measures, not a bird for me
> But the name of a bird and the name of a nameless air
> I have never—shall never hear. And yet beneath
> The stillness of everything gone, and being still,
> Being and sitting still, something resides,
> Some skreaking and skrittering residuum,
> And grates these evasions of the nightingale
> Though I never—shall never hear that bird.
> And the stillness is in the key, all of it is,
> The stillness is all in the key of that desolate sound.

Both "Owl's Clover" and "The Man with the Blue Guitar"
served the useful purpose of helping him redefine his subject,
but neither was a success. "Owl's Clover," with the possible
exception of "The Old Woman and the Statue," suffered from
a weakness he put his finger on in "The Irrational Element
in Poetry," in which he described, in part, the concept behind
it—a concept not so different from the concept behind his
other work, but somehow viewed from the wrong end of the
telescope:

> . . . I wanted to apply my own sensibility to some-
> thing perfectly matter-of-fact [*i.e.*, the Depression,
> the "anxieties and tensions" of 1935–36]. The result
> would be a disclosure of my own sensibility or in-
> dividuality . . . certainly to myself.

And he went on to say,

> While there is nothing automatic about the poem,

nevertheless it has an automatic aspect in the sense
that it is what I wanted it to be without knowing
before it was written what I wanted it to be, even
though I knew before it was written what I wanted to
do. If each of us is a biological mechanism, each poet
is a poetic mechanism. To the extent that what he
produces is mechanical: that is to say, beyond his
power to change, it is irrational. Perhaps I do not
mean wholly beyond his power to change, for he
might, by an effort of the will, change it. With that
in mind, I mean beyond likelihood of change so long
as he is being himself. This happens in the case of
every poet.

He had, as he suspected, mistaken what he called the "true
subject" for "the poetry of the subject"; torn between a desire
for a "constant" and "orderly" development in his own work
and the feeling that he was perhaps a poet "brought up in
an artificial school," he had, like "the Mallarmiste," become
"a proletarian novelist." He had fallen prey to the pressures
of fashion. Tired of his old poems, he was casting about for a
means of renewal—but his error in the long run was no greater than similar errors made by other poets of even greater
scope. Moreover, he was able to learn something from his
attempt, as "The Noble Rider and the Sound of Words" and
"Notes toward a Supreme Fiction" well prove.

The antitheses of "The Man with the Blue Guitar," at
least in the first few sections of the poem, are evidence of
an attempt to develop his subject in the orderly fashion he
thought he had glimpsed in "Owl's Clover," but the seesawing
back and forth between what the man with the blue guitar
said and what "they" said very soon becomes monotonous, and
the figures intended to bear the weight of the argument of
the poem remain either bleakly two-dimensional or so el-
liptical, like many of the "aphorisms" in "Like Decorations
in a Nigger Cemetery," that the effort to untangle their
"meaning" seems to be more than it is worth. "The amorist/
Adjective aflame," or "the lion in the lute/Before the lion

locked in stone" is only a little less irritating than the jargon of nineteenth-century aesthetics, and the equivalent of its "golden oblong." The three rejected sections of the poem (printed in *Opus Posthumous*), which may have been written in the "most slap-dash way," are as good as anything in the finished poem; and they have the added virtue of "seeming but a moment's thought," improvisations as natural to their author as one has a right to expect. Their holiday brightness, however, would have clashed with the tone of the rest.

What he once called "the difficult thinking" of these two long poems freed him for the short pieces that followed. They began with the "Canonica," the twelve poems in the opening pages of *Parts of a World*, including "Poetry Is a Destructive Force," "The Poems of Our Climate," "Prelude to Objects," "Study of Two Pears," "The Glass of Water," and "Add This to Rhetoric," all of which concerned the "problems of realization"; and "Parochial Theme," "Dry Loaf," "Idiom of the Hero" and "On the Road Home," in which the poet's relation to a world menaced by an uncertain future was reexamined. In two of the poems, "The Man on the Dump" and "The Latest Freed Man," the sense of momentary fulfillment, "when change composes, too," and life seems "complete in itself," reasserted itself: between one "disgust" and another—between winter and summer—"One feels the purifying change. One rejects/The trash" of a stale past and an undefined future; but whether it is "peace" or a "philosopher's honeymoon" that "one finds/On the dump," the poem does not say:

> Is it to sit among mattresses of the dead,
> Bottles, pots, shoes and grass and murmur *aptest eve:*
> Is it to hear the blatter of grackles and say
> *Invisible priest;* is it to eject, to pull
> The day to pieces and cry *stanza my stone?*
> Where was it one first heard of the truth? The the.

He had asked a similar question twenty years earlier, in "The Indigo Glass in the Grass," a "trifle" he had wanted to sub-

stitute for one of the poems in "Pecksniffiana," but there he
had been looking for something to "contain the world," something "real," and had been more certain of the answer:

> Which is real—
> This bottle of indigo glass in the grass,
> Or the bench with the pot of geraniums, the stained
>   mattress and the washed overalls drying in
>   the sun?
> Which of these truly contains the world?
> Neither one, nor the two together.

Though he already knew that "nothing exists by itself," he
had not had to face up to a world which seemed steadily
growing shabbier and more uncertain; and the possibility of
containment still seemed possible. What he had grown to see
was the possibility of a force to sustain and to bring into a
vital relationship both the poet and the external world around
him, not only as a means of self-preservation but also as a
means of preserving and giving value to that external world.
One could not, from his point of view, have a nobler task;
and for him the moments when "everything" was "bulging
and blazing and big in itself," when "the pensive man," who
was also the "connoisseur of chaos" could see "that eagle
float/For which the intricate Alps are a single nest," were
what gave life its sanction. At the end of "The Noble Rider
and the Sound of Words," he said:

> Late last year Epstein exhibited some of his flower
> paintings at the Leicester Galleries in London. A
> commentator in *Apollo* said: *"How with this rage can
> beauty hold a plea* . . . The quotation from Shake-
> speare's 65th sonnet prefaces the catalogue. . . . It
> would be apropos to any other flower paintings than
> Mr. Epstein's. His make no pretence to fragility.
> They shout, explode all over the picture space and
> generally oppose the rage of the world with such a
> rage of form and colour as no flower in nature or
> pigment has done since Van Gogh."

What ferocious beauty the line from Shakespeare puts on when used under such circumstances! While it has its modulation of despair, it holds its plea and its plea is noble. There is no element more conspicuously absent from contemporary poetry than nobility. There is no element that poets have sought after, more curiously and more piously, certain of its obscure existence. Its voice is one of the inarticulate voices which it is their business to overhear and to record. The nobility of rhetoric is, of course, a lifeless nobility. Pareto's epigram that history is a cemetery of aristocracies easily becomes another: that poetry is a cemetery of nobilities. For the sensitive poet, conscious of negations, nothing is more difficult than the affirmations of nobility and yet there is nothing that he requires of himself more persistently, since in them and in their kind alone, are to be found those sanctions that are the reasons for his being and for that occasional ecstasy, or ecstatic freedom of the mind, which is his special privilege.

It is hard to think of a thing more out of time than nobility. Looked at plainly it seems false and dead and ugly. To look at it at all makes us realize sharply that in our present, in the presence of our reality, the past looks false and is, therefore, dead and is, therefore, ugly; and we turn away from it as from something repulsive and particularly from the characteristic that it has a way of assuming: something that was noble in its day, grandeur that was, the rhetorical once. But as a wave is a force and not the water of which it is composed, which is never the same, so nobility is a force and not the manifestations of which it is composed, which are never the same. Possibly this description of it as a force will do more than anything else I can have said about it to reconcile you to it. It is not an artifice that the mind has added to human nature. The mind has added nothing to human nature. It is a violence from within that protects us from a violence without. It is the imagination pressing back against the pres-

sure of reality. It seems, in the last analysis, to have
something to do with our self-preservation; and that,
no doubt, is why the expression of it, the sound of
its words, helps us to live our lives.

This is as eloquent a testimony to the belief in poetry as one
of the great humanities as any we are likely to have in our
time, generous and free of self-seeking and self-aggrandizement. Whether it had its roots in Santayana, or Charles
Mauron, or Kierkegaard, what it may owe to the "two or
three dozen books" on his table that he "had never looked
at before," and that in any case cannot be identified, would
seem to be beside the point. The real test of its worth—of
what it means—would seem to be its power to persuade one
as much of its profound humaneness as well as of its right-
ness. After reading the books on his table, Stevens said, "I
have concluded to say my say on my own account, with the
least possible reference to others. One must stand by one's
own ideas, or not at all."

The same must be said of the poems which fulfill even
more precisely than "Notes toward a Supreme Fiction" the
conditions by which the fiction itself, whether it be poetry
or the poetry of life, is to be recognized: it must be abstract
—that is, it must be limited and one's own, for it cannot be
otherwise; it must change—if only in the repetitions and re-
currences that give the world and the human mind identity
and also threaten it with extinction; and it must give pleasure—whether it is no more than the sense of well-being that,
in taking account of the "modulation of despair" common to
all experience, nevertheless is its own justification or is one
of the momentary "secretions of insight" in which, without
egotism or vanity, we seem to be at the center of the sphere.
Eliot called it "the still point of the turning world"; but Eliot's
world is vain and deceiving. And although Stevens's sphere
is an illusion, too, a metaphor, finally,

                        It is
        As if the central poem became the world,

And the world the central poem, each one the mate
Of the other, as if summer was a spouse,
Espoused each morning, each long afternoon,
And the mate of summer: her mirror and her look,
Her only place and person, a self of her
That speaks, denouncing separate selves, both one.
The essential poem begets the others. The light
Of it is not a light apart, up-hill.

The central poem is the poem of the whole,
The poem of the composition of the whole,
The composition of blue sea and of green,
Of blue light and of green, as lesser poems,
And the miraculous multiplex of lesser poems,
Not merely into a whole, but a poem of
The whole, the essential compact of the parts,
The roundness that pulls tight the final ring . . .

In the beginning the "Notes" were to have "developed" the intuition of the supreme fiction in an orderly fashion; but they ended by "playing" with the idea, as he told Henry Church. They "are a miscellany in which it would be difficult to collect the theory latent in them," "illustrations," or, more simply, poems. The reader for whom unity is of the essence of poetry will find the "Notes" deficient; but the reader willing to take any one of the thirty sections and the epilogue, at least to begin with, on its own terms—which means that each poem must be regarded as a whole rather than as a counter fixed in a clearly articulate sequence or discourse—is likely to be better rewarded. Their "order," or the order they propose, is organic, but not to be grasped by the kind of Procrustean exegesis which has been imposed upon them. The poem iterates and reiterates again and again its own way of "delineating" its subject, to use Stevens's own word:

It is he. The man
In that old coat, those sagging pantaloons,

It is of him, ephebe, to make, to confect
The final elegance, not to console
Nor sanctify, but plainly to propound.
. . . .
The poem goes from the poet's gibberish to
The gibberish of the vulgate and back again.
Does it move to and fro or is it of both

At once? Is it a luminous flittering
Or the concentration of a cloudy day?
. . . .
He imposes orders as he thinks of them,
As the fox and snake do. It is a brave affair.
Next he builds capitols and in their corridors,

Whiter than wax, sonorous, fame as it is,
He establishes statues of reasonable men,
Who surpassed the most literate owl, the most erudite

Of elephants. But to impose is not
To discover. To discover an order as of
A season, to discover summer and know it,

To discover winter and know it well, to find,
Not to impose, not to have reasoned at all,
Out of nothing to have come on major weather,

It is possible, possible, possible. It must
Be possible. It must be that in time
The real will from its crude compoundings come . . .

Whatever the "Notes" owe to Hegel or Henri Focillon's *Life
of Forms in Art*, they are first and last an attempt by the
poet to "say his say on his own account, with the least possible reference to others"; their final authority and center of
reference are the "commonplaces" of experience, not an order

imposed upon them. The eight lines that precede "It Must Be Abstract" make this clear:

> And for what, except for you, do I feel love?
> Do I press the extremest book of the wisest man
> Close to me, hidden in me day and night?
> In the uncertain light of single, certain truth,
> Equal in living changingness to the light
> In which I meet you, in which we sit at rest,
> For a moment in the central of our being,
> The vivid transparence that you bring is peace.

The "you" is the supreme fiction itself—the "enigma," as he called it, as well as poetry and the world. So seen, all that follows does move with a kind of increasing fullness to its conclusion, but it moves with the freedom of love and faith, of

> a vital affair, not an affair of the heart (as it may be in one's first poems), but an affair of the whole being (as in one's last poems), a fundamental affair of life, or, rather, an affair of fundamental life; so that one's cry of O Jerusalem becomes little by little a cry to something a little nearer and nearer until at last one cries out to a living name, a living place, a living thing, and in crying out confesses openly to all the bitter secretions of experience.

Like any faith, like love, it asks essentially a yielding to it. Stevens was not writing here of himself, but of John Crowe Ransom, six years after completing the "Notes." But nothing, except perhaps the "last poems" themselves, sums up his life as a poet; and the last poems were still to come.

IV. THE LAST YEARS (1945–1955)

MORE THAN HALF of the letters in the volume edited by his daughter Holly belong to the last fourteen years of Stevens's life; and of these almost four hundred were written after 1946. Together with the poems and essays that span the same period—nearly half of all he published—they comprise a full record of the life of his mind. They make any biography, in one sense, superfluous, and they reveal how completely he succeeded, especially during the last ten years, in putting "the same degree of intentness into his poetry as, for example, the traveler into his adventure, the painter into his painting." Yet he did not live "the literary life," nor did he have a desire to do so. In a letter to José Rodríguez Feo, written in 1945, which began with a comment on his interest in discovering "how much alike" he and his young friend were, and continued with a brief discussion of his feeling that Stendhal would survive Flaubert "because Stendhal is a point of reference for the mature, while Flaubert is a point of reference for the artist, and perhaps for the immature," and a paragraph expressing his approval of being able to say "Pooh!" to "the snobbery of the young man [Charles Henri Ford] who knows a little more about painting than his neighbor, in the sense that he knows an artist or two," he had gone on to speak of his promise to send some poems for *Origenes:*

The poem, or poems, that I shall send to you will have to be written during the summer, because I have been busy with something else [genealogy, "Description without Place," arrangements for the Cummington Press edition of *Esthétique du Mal*] and, besides, I almost always dislike anything that I do that doesn't fly in the window. Perhaps this has some bearing on what you call "the monotony of elegance". To live in Cuba, to think a little in the morning and afterward to work in the garden for an hour or two, then to have lunch and to read all afternoon and then, with your wife or someone else's wife, fill the house with fresh roses, to play a little Berlioz (this is the current combination at home: Berlioz and roses) might very well create all manner of doubts after a week or two. But when you are a little older, and have your business or your job to look after, and when there is quite enough to worry about all the time, and when you don't have time to think and the weeds grow in the garden a good deal more savagely than you could ever have supposed, and you no longer read because it doesn't seem worth while, but you do at the end of the day play a record or two, that is something quite different. Reality is the great *fond*, and it is because it is that the purely literary amounts to so little. Moreover, in the world of actuality, in spite of all I have just said, one is always living a little out of it. There is a precious sentence in Henry James, for whom everyday life was not much more than the mere business of living, but, all the same, he separated himself from it. The sentence is . . .

"To live *in* the world of creation—to get into it and stay in it—to frequent it and haunt it—to *think* intensely and fruitfully—to woo combinations and inspirations into being by a depth and continuity of attention and meditation—this is the only thing."

This paragraph sums up, as well as possible—which with Stevens is never so well as it may seem to be at first—his attitude toward the relation of the parts of his life to his life

as a whole. Clearly, to "live *in* the world of creation" was
what satisfied him most fully; and many of his poems reveal
him wooing "combinations and inspirations into being by a
depth and continuity of attention and meditation" that is a
continuing source of wonder. But there are others, as Randall
Jarrell· has said, which make an amazingly "interesting rhetoric
out of just fooling around: turning things upside-down, looking
at them from under the sofa, considering them (and their
observer) curiously enough to make the reader protest, 'That
were to consider it too curiously.'"

The paragraph also tells a good deal about the relation of
his daily routine—of the discipline of going to the office—to
the indulgence "at the end of the day," which was not only
a contrast but a complement; and it suggests that what "you
do at the end of the day" acquires its great value partly because one has to wait for it, that "the privilege of the mind"
is all the better for the release it brings. What has been
stored up or collected in pools during the day, in the "world
of actuality," is what "flies in the window": the "evening's
thought" that is "like a day of clear weather"; the poem,
whether it is the poem that gets itself written down or is
simply the experience that a poem should resemble. And
perhaps because "in the world of actuality . . . one is always
living a little out of it," he was always living *"in* the world
of creation," even when he was sitting at his desk, busy with
"the mere business of living" or making a living. From this
point of view, he could quite honestly say that he was not a
divided man; and one can understand why he had given up
his "boyish" notion that "things progressed by contrasts, that
there was a law of contrasts," and had come to the conclusion,
as he told Hi Simons, that "this was building the world out of
blocks."

> Afterwards I came to think more of the energizing
> that comes from mere interplay, interaction. Thus the
> various faculties of the mind co-exist and interact,

and there is as much delight in this mere co-existence as a man and a woman find in each other's company. . . . Cross-reflections, modifications, counter-balances, complements, giving and taking are illimitable. They make things inter-dependent, and their inter-dependence sustains them and gives them pleasure. While it may be the cause of other things, I am thinking of it as a source of pleasure, and therefore I repeat that there is an exquisite pleasure and harmony in these interrelations, circuits.

This conclusion had also much to do with the figure of "the imagination pressing back against the pressure of reality," and with that "third reader" of any text, whom he delineates in "Effects of Analogy,"

. . . one for whom the story and the other meaning should come together like two aspects that combine to produce a third or, if they do not combine, inter-act, so that one influences the other and produces an effect similar in kind to the prismatic formations that occur about us in nature in the case of reflections and refractions.

Such was the effect in nature that he had noticed in the Gulf of Mexico in 1923, and had superbly captured in "Sea Surface Full of Clouds"; and such were the effects he had striven to capture in the more abstracted poetry—whether of the "first idea" or "the painter's problem of realization," the "real" or the "unreal"—that had followed. Even the "preliminary minutiae" of *Harmonium* had shown an intuition of this interplay, not only in such obvious examples as "Tea at the Palaz of Hoon," "The Snow Man," and the various "anecdotes," but also in "Peter Quince at the Clavier" and "Sunday Morning," and so elaborate a bit of spoofing about the difficulty of seeing the world as it is and of thinking one thing—or more than one thing—long enough to think it at all, as "Metaphors of a Magnifico":

Twenty men crossing a bridge,
Into a village,
Are twenty men crossing twenty bridges,
Into twenty villages,
Or one man
Crossing a single bridge into a village.

This is old song
That will not declare itself . . .

Twenty men crossing a bridge,
Into a village,
Are
Twenty men crossing a bridge
Into a village.

That will not declare itself
Yet is certain as meaning . . .

The boots of the men clump
On the boards of the bridge.
The first white wall of the village
Rises through fruit-trees.
Of what was it I was thinking?
So the meaning escapes.

The first white wall of the village . . .
The fruit trees. . . .

The world was indeed what one thinks of it, as much as
what one makes of it; and it was, as he said in the "Adagia,"
"the only thing fit to think about," just as "words [were]
everything else in the world."

A life so devoid of outward drama and excitement or interest, despite a handful of anecdotes, such as the one concerning his "fight" with Hemingway at Key West, or the story
of his reply to Robert Frost, who had complained that Stevens's
poems had "no subject" ("The trouble with yours, Robert, is

that they have subjects"), made it possible to concentrate his attention on poetry in order to make a life of his own. To be, or try to be, "a contemporary man who writes poetry" was his way of being a poet in America, which has been largely without any tradition to support the idea of a man of letters. The ordinary disappointments and difficulties he suffered seem not to have been in any way unusual. He was a success in business. He was a great poet. It is just here, however, that he does seem to have been unusual; and the care he took for a long time to keep business and poetry separate in every way is in itself evidence of his recognition that in his own way, like Thoreau, he had more than one life to live, even though, in the long run, all his lives had to be one.

The record of the last years—the letters, the poems and essays, the widening circle of friends, the awards and honors which he thought had nothing to do with poetry but were nonetheless testimony of the esteem in which his contemporaries held him—is something more than a success story. So far as the poetry is concerned, "Notes toward a Supreme Fiction" "delineated" his "true subject," but did not go beyond it; and although the poems that followed did not pursue the topic further in "a number of books . . . a THEORY OF SUPREME FICTION . . . a BOOK OF SPECIMENS, etc., etc.," which he told Henry Church he might write if he "had nothing else in the world to do except to sit on a fence and think about things," they moved with increasing certitude to their climax in the poems of "The Rock," the final section of the *Collected Poems*. The essays carried the argument of "The Noble Rider and the Sound of Words" and "The Figure of the Youth as Virile Poet" no further; but they enriched and clarified some aspects of his thought in ways that provide some of the best commentary on the poems that we are likely to have. The last of them, "The Whole Man: Perspectives, Horizons," which is also the briefest and the most clearly an article of faith, may be of little interest to his explicators, but it is by all means the most self-revelatory, and it defines the sort of synthesis he had come at the end to believe:

It is possible to conceive a neo-Platonic republic in which technicians would be political and moral neuters. In such a republic, one class would be the class of all-round men: the general thinkers, men capable of different sights, the sturdy fathers of that very republic and the authors of its political and moral declarations. Since most of us are technicians on at least one side or, say, to some extent, those in whom we reposed the profoundest confidence would actually be few, perhaps a group composed of men with minds like the rapacious and benign mind of Professor Whitehead. To be ruled by thought, in reality to govern ourselves by the truth or to be able to feel that we were being governed by the truth, would be a great satisfaction, as things go. The great modern faith, the key to an understanding of our times, is faith in the truth and particularly in the idea that the truth is attainable, and that a free civilization based on the truth, in general and in detail, is no less attainable.

"The great objective," he said in the "Adagia," "is the truth, not only of the poem but of poetry." But poetic truth was not ethics or the record of one's life; it was, rather, "the statement of a relation between a man and the world," and in this sense, the metaphor of his life. The letters of the last fifteen years, in a profusion that is almost overwhelming, provide a running commentary on his constant and constantly shifting interests and day-to-day thinking. They give insight into the meaning of many of the most characteristic turns of phrase and habits of mind which identify him as a poet, and they show a deepening generosity of spirit, a tolerance of "the dreadful sundry of this world," that is at first surprising in a man who had once said that "egotism is at the bottom of everything everybody does." Yet they are completely in character.

He welcomed the routine of the office—because he liked it, and had "use for the money"—even after he reached the mandatory retirement age of seventy; and one of the reasons he did not accept the invitation of Harvard to occupy the Charles Eliot Norton Chair in 1955 was simply that "to take the greater part of a year . . . would be only too likely to precipitate the retirement" he wanted "so much to put off." "What is more," he added, "I cannot imagine taking up the routine of the office again, at my age, after being away from it for a long period of time." But "work at the office" stood increasingly often "in the way . . ."; it was "that or something else . . . so that," he wrote to Norman Holmes Pearson in April 1954, "often when I reach home and finish the Hartford Times it seems to be more interesting just to lean back and take a nap than to do anything else." A few months earlier, he had written to Mrs. Church:

> This present note marks my return to the outside world after what is best described as a convention of our principal men, from all over the country, last week. I sat in a smoke-ball (of cigars, pipes, cigarettes) day after day, listening to platitudes propounded as if they were head-splitting perceptions. That's over and we look forward to a good year. A few nights' sleep in fresh air have revived me, mais mon Dieu! I want now a little spell of quiet reading by some polished person. On Sunday I picked up a new book of poems by one of my friends and was shocked by his lack of care and feeling. I read little poetry and was much let down by this work on the part of a man whom I had regarded—without really reading him—as, like a minor, modern, poetic Cicero—to be a writer to delight all men of taste. His book is a miscellany without an axis.

It was perhaps because his own way of life had given his poetry its axis that he remained of two minds about retirement; and certainly until his final illness, his routine at the office did not interfere with his productivity, although it may have limited his own sense of his achievement more than his readers can realize. Roy Harvey Pearce, however, has pointed

out that the cost of the "really done things" (a phrase borrowed from James's Preface to *The Golden Bowl*) was "suffering and pain," which, it should be added, hardly appear
in the poetry. What was "given up" was some sense of the
ordinary world in which most of his readers have to live.
"The reward," as Pearce has said, "for Stevens as for James,
is knowledge and individuality—and a measure of freedom."
It was the reward of "the elegantly creative act," which he
knew had its limitations: "Esthetique," he said, "is the measure of a civilization: not the sole measure, but a measure."
And it was not simply a matter of deliberate choice on his
part; it was equally a matter of temperament.

The acceptance he had almost arrogantly belittled when
Harmonium was in the making left him no less demanding of
himself when it did come, but it helped him master his diffidence about being a poet. In mastering life, or the "mere
business of living," he became increasingly aware of his own
good fortune; in mastering his poetry, he found, somewhat to
his surprise, that he could write of things which he had supposed were outside the limits of his own sensibility: when
he was asked to write the Phi Beta Kappa poem for Columbia
University in 1954, it was possible to "use some of the words,"
at least, of the "birthday theme"; and although he had been
left free to choose his own theme for "An Ordinary Evening
in New Haven," written in honor of the thousandth meeting
of the Connecticut Academy of Arts and Sciences in 1949,
he chose a topic suitable for the occasion. "Recitation after
Dinner," composed for the Saint Nicholas Society, was also
an occasional piece, as was the rather curious prose essay,
"A Ceremony," which he apparently wrote for his own amuse-
ment—there is no record, at least, of its having been used at
any meeting of the society. His widening correspondence
brought more things "flying in the window": a phrase in a
letter from José Rodríguez Feo, some lines from a poem by
Thomas McGreevy; and as always, the occasional picture from
Paris, sent to him by Mlle. Vidal, renewed his imagination
and the habit of meditation, most notably in "Angel Sur-

rounded by Paysans," in which the transforming power of his mind is most vividly shown.

"When one is young," he wrote in the "Adagia," "everything is physical; when one is old everything is psychic"; and, even more pointedly, "The poet is a god, or, the young poet is a god. The old poet is a tramp," like the humane and lonely figure described at the end of "It Must Be Abstract" in "Notes toward a Supreme Fiction." And as his mind mellowed, the language of his poetry grew simpler, less finicking and fastidious, but at its best no less precise than it had always been. The wit of the "Notes" and the poems written thereafter became gentler; the surface of the poems was more discursive, in some ways, and less dazzling, yet neither so abstract nor so frequently embellished with the details that he had included for his own pleasure, as he once said it had been his habit to do. Indeed, although his style remained his own, it changed enough to give substance to his remark that "a change of style is a change of subject," for example, in the poems in distichs that counterpoint the more usual poems in tristichs characteristic of his late work. One sees the change in "A Completely New Set of Objects," written about the annual festival on the Schuylkill River "down which paraded canoes and boats lighted at night with candled Chinese lanterns," which he remembered from his boyhood:

From a Schuylkill in mid-earth there came emerging
Flotillas, willed and wanted, bearing in them

Shadows of friends, of those he knew, each bringing
From the water in which he believed and out of desire

Things made by mid-terrestrial, mid-human
Makers without knowing, or intending, uses.

These figures verdant with time's buried verdure
Came paddling their canoes, a thousand thousand,

Carrying such shapes, of such alleviation,
That the beholder knew their subtle purpose,

Knew well the shapes were the exactest shaping
Of a vast people old in meditation . . .

Under Tinicum or small Cohansey,
The fathers of the makers may lie and weather.

It certainly did not occur to him that "A Completely New
Set of Objects," or some of the other poems similarly grounded
in his own past—"Dutch Graves in Bucks County," "Thinking
of a Relation between the Images of Metaphors," "Late Hymn
from the Myrrh Mountain," "The Old Lutheran Bells at
Home," and "Credences of Summer," which one commentator
has said "seems written in reminiscence of a hike over Mount
Penn, from whose Tower Stevens could see 'Oley, too rich for
enigmas'"—would please the "oldsters" who had their own
memories of that lost world to sustain them; but the mere fact
that the places, persons, and events which these poems recalled and re-created belonged as much to "actuality" as to
the "invented world" of his own mind gave them an unexpected pathos. Metamorphosed by memory, they required no
further modification. They had a human interest more powerful than anything that might be evoked by "the hero," "the
MacCullough," "the Canon Aspirin," or "the poet," and his
other archetypal characters, or any "imagined" Segovia or
Basel, although "the ultimate elegance" would remain "the
imagined land" and "the world imagined" endured as "the
final good."

It would be easy to say, as some of his critics have implied,
that the life he mastered was neither a difficult nor a complex
one, and that the sense of tragedy is lacking in his work. On
its most superficial level, the criticism amounts to little more
than their disapproval of his conservatism in politics or his taste
in painting. William Carlos Williams once observed that Stevens
had made his decision not to travel because he was satisfied

with the experience of the world he had accumulated as a young man, almost as if to assert that the poetry suffered from a kind of needless provincialism that travel would have corrected; and the fact that Stevens never travelled abroad has seemed as incredible as the fact that he wrote poetry was to some of his business associates even after he had been elected to the National Institute of Arts and Letters and had won the Bollingen Prize. He wrote to José Rodríguez Feo in 1949, with his customary mixture of seriousness and facetiousness,

> This spring I have quite a number of invitations to talk here and there but I don't see the connection between writing poetry and delivering lectures. I am not a lecturer and I have no intentions of doing that sort of thing except in cases in which I very much want to. It would be interesting to meet people in colleges, but then one never meets them at a lecture. If, for example, General Eisenhower should ask me to come down to Columbia and have a few highballs with him, that would be worth while. Yet it may be that, even if he did, when I got down there he would want to show me moving pictures of Hitler's funeral or something.

His comment to Marius Bewley on the 1952 elections was equally cavalier:

> But Stevenson was not my man. Even in the case of Eisenhower, however, I should be cautious because we ought to have a little prose in the White House after all the poor poetry, to say nothing of the music.

Yet he never objected to committing himself seriously on those matters of genuine concern to him, including those rather pretentious bits of elitism conducted by the *Partisan Review* disguised as "The Situation in American Writing: Seven Questions," in 1939, and "The State of American Writing: a Symposium," in 1948. To the double-barrelled and

heavily loaded question, "Have you considered the question
of your attitude towards the possible entry of the United
States into the next world war? What do you think the responsibilities of writers in general are when and if war
comes?" he replied seriously and thoughtfully, with less self-
consciousness if not quite such high-mindedness as many of
his fellow writers, including Gertrude Stein, Allen Tate, James
T. Farrell, Katherine Anne Porter, and Lionel Trilling:

> I don't think that the United States should enter
> into the next world war, if there is to be another,
> unless it does so with the idea of dominating the
> world that comes out of it, or unless it is required
> to enter it in self-defense. The question respecting the
> responsibility of writers in war is a very theoretical
> question respecting an extremely practical state of
> affairs. A war is a military state of affairs, not a
> literary one. Conceding that the propagandists don't
> agree, does it matter that they don't agree? The role
> of the writer in war remains the fundamental role of
> the writer intensified and concentrated.

To commit himself more specifically would have been out
of character; the role of prophet was not for him the role
of the poet. But he did try during World War II to keep his
attention on what he thought was relevant to his work; and
although the war seemed to him primarily an instance of "the
periodical failure of politics," and therefore irrelevant to his
interests as a poet, it made itself felt from time to time in
his work, as in the epilogue to "Notes toward a Supreme
Fiction":

> Soldier, there is a war between the mind
> And sky, between thought and day and night. It is
> For that the poet is always in the sun,
>
> Patches the moon together in his room
> To his Virgilian cadences, up down,
> Up down. It is a war that never ends.

Yet it depends on yours. The two are one.
They are a plural, a right and left, a pair,
Two parallels that meet if only in

The meeting of their shadows or that meet
In a book in a barrack, a letter from Malay.
But your war ends. And after it you return

With six meats and twelve wines or else without
To walk another room . . . Monsieur and comrade,
The soldier is poor without the poet's lines,

His petty syllabi, the sounds that stick,
Inevitably modulating, in the blood.
And war for war, each has its gallant kind.

How simply the fictive hero becomes the real;
How gladly with proper words the soldier dies,
If he must, or lives on the bread of faithful speech.

Despite its humaneness, his poem did not approach Frost's great sonnet of World War I, "A Soldier," nor Marianne Moore's "In Distrust of Merits" and "We Call Them the Brave"; but it was his own "faithful speech."

The end of the war restored to him communication with the Europe of his imagination. As soon as he was able to do so, he was buying pictures again: Bombois, Detthow, Oudot, Cavaillès, Tal Coat, one at a time, enjoying the choosing and anticipation of their arrival in Hartford even more, at times, than the paintings themselves. Paris also meant books, albums of lithographs by Marquet, exhibition catalogs, arrangements to have his own books bound by René Aussourd, picture postcards of Tarbes, to help him "realize" the town that had given its title to Jean Paulhan's book, *Les Fleurs de Tarbes*, and that interested him more than the book itself. He wrote to Mrs. Church at Ville d'Avray, savoring her news of France when she was there during the summers, and corresponding with and seeing something of her in New York in the winter. Thomas McGreevy, who had made Ireland large in his imagination, also made him a "large-scale correspondent." They met, not at the Avery Memorial in Hartford where McGreevy came in 1954 to attend a conference of museum directors, but at Mrs. Church's apartment in New York. "I was amazed," Stevens wrote her, after an earlier visit to the Avery to meet Mr. and Mrs. James Johnson Sweeney a few weeks before McGreevy was to arrive, "to see how many people there are in Hartford whom I have never seen before. . . . and I am afraid it would only embarrass me to look him up at the Bond [Hotel] . . ."

He continued to write, and promise, poems to old and new magazines. The thirty-fifth anniversary issue of *Poetry* contained "The Ultimate Poem Is Abstract" and "Bouquet of Roses in Sunlight," with its warm, almost intimate stanza at the conclusion:

> We are two that use these roses as we are,
> In seeing them. This is what makes them seem
> So far beyond the rhetorician's touch.

There were poems in *Accent, Horizon, Wake, Halcyon, Voices, American Letters, Botteghe Oscure,* the *Nation, Poetry London,* and in the *Kenyon Review,* to which he sent "The Auroras of Autumn." He lectured at Harvard, where he read "Three Academic Pieces." He wrote tributes to John Crowe Ransom on his sixtieth birthday and to Marianne Moore for a special issue of the *Quarterly Review of Literature;* memorial tributes to Henry Church and Paul Rosenfeld; and read the Bergen Lecture at Yale. "An Ordinary Evening in New Haven" occupied most of his attention during the spring and early summer of 1949—the time of year he had always found propitious for sustained effort. He told Bernard Heringman:

> . . . here my interest is to try to get as close to the
> ordinary, the commonplace and the ugly as it is pos-

sible for a poet to get. It is not a question of grim
reality but of plain reality. The object is of course to
purge oneself of anything false. I have been doing this
since the beginning of March and intend to keep
studying the subject and work on it until I am quite
through with it. This is not in any sense a turning
away from the ideas of Credences of Summer: it is
a development of those ideas. That sort of thing might
ultimately lead to another phase of what you call a
seasonal sequence but certainly it would have nothing
to do with the weather: it would have to do with the
drift of one's ideas.

Yet weather was of import to the poems; as he said in the
"Adagia," "Weather is a sense of nature. Poetry is a sense."
As a metaphor for "the drift of his ideas," his "ordinary
evening" was intended to create "a new reality from which
the original"—the actuality—appeared "to be unreal"; in his
"thinking," perceptions, as he liked to say, were "essential."
When he said that his seasonal sequence had nothing to do
with the weather, he meant, primarily, that it had nothing
to do with "the seasons of the soul" in any traditional allegorical way: winter was not an equivalent for death, nor
was summer a symbol for maturity. He was no more an al-
legorist at seventy than he had been in 1898, when he noted
in his journal, "Coming home I saw the sun go down behind
a veil of grime. It was rather terrifying I confess from an
allegorical point of view. But that is usually the case with
allegory."

He did not read much philosophy, in any case, not even
aesthetics: "the little . . . that I have read," he told Heringman, "has been read very much in the spirit in which Henry
Church used to read it. He said that he read philosophy for
forty years. It seemed that he read it as a substitute for fiction." Even allowing for his desire to avoid being tagged as
a Platonist, or a humanist, or a disciple of Santayana, and
his quite natural resistance to acknowledging any great indebtedness to the "ideas" of Mallarmé or Coleridge, there

can be no doubt that he felt about philosophy as he often felt about poetry: "It is necessary to any originality to have the courage to be an amateur." "A Collect of Philosophy," the paper he read for the Moody Lecture at the University of Chicago in 1951, concerned "the poetry of philosophy . . . the poetic nature of philosophical conceptions. For instance, the idea that because perception is sensory we never see reality immediately but always the moment after is a a poetic idea. We live in mental representations of the past." Like a good many other poets, he rebelled against the confusion of highmindedness or metaphysics and poetry; and he was constantly turning the tables on religion and philosophy in order to validate the significance of poetry. "Poetry is a means of redemption," he said in the "Adagia"; and "After one has abandoned a belief in god, poetry is that essence which takes its place as life's redemption." So, too, he said, "Perhaps it is of more value to infuriate philosophers than to go along with them"; and, in keeping with his desire to assure poetry of its nobility, he defined politics as "the struggle for existence." If he did not contradict Aristotle's opinion that the gift for metaphor was more important to the poet than any other gift, he nevertheless stated his version of the idea in more complex terms: "Reality is a cliché from which we escape by metaphor. It is only *au pays de la metaphore qu'on est poète.*" And if, as here, the content of the adage seems hardly to justify the elaborateness of its form, it is important to remember that for him the most significant task of the poet was to make everything his own. Indeed, in writing of "A Collect of Philosophy" to Mrs. Church, he said,

> I am sure the subject is a good one. Tom Sergeant, an eminent Bostonian, said that philosophy is a thing in which the philosopher exhibits his natural amiability. I like that attitude. To say that philosophers are poets, after all, does them no harm and at the same time somehow magnifies poetry, so that one comes to see it in all its greatness and power, in spite of all the bad or silly poetry. I thought that that was my best

point: the disclosure of modern man as one to be
measured by the greatness of poetry or rather by the
idea of the greatness of poetry.

Thus the reality with which he begins "An Ordinary Evening in New Haven," "the eye's plain version," is quite literally "a thing apart,/The vulgate of experience." At the
same time it is his own sense of that "plain version," what
he has by nature, that makes him aware of his individuality.
Only in these late poems does "we" become as important as
"I" or "one." Here his focus on actuality or everyday life allows him to see figures other than his own in his poetic landscape. Perhaps this means nothing more than that his world
had grown large enough to allow him to see the world imagined and the world of fact as one. Discursive as many of its
thirty-one sections in the familiar tristichs are, they are something more than the facile effort of "an extremist in an exercise" which some critics have found them to be. Their
accessibility, indeed, is nothing against them; and if they lack
the density of "Notes toward a Supreme Fiction," or "Credences of Summer," and do not quite suggest the physical
world given body in those poems and in "Esthétique du Mal,"
their tonalities are surer: one catches the emotional inflections
more readily than in the preceding long poems, in which the
ironies and ambiguities are sometimes so dazzling that it is
difficult to grasp the modulations of feeling. Frank Kermode
has pointed out that "An Ordinary Evening in New Haven"
is full of "as-ifs"; for this very reason, it lends itself less easily
to the kind of explication which makes it appear that Stevens
is a philosopher and not a poet. And whatever its weaknesses,
particularly for the sophisticated reader who wants and can
accept the challenge of meeting a poet wholly on his own
ground—which may be, after all, impossible—this last long
poem lays the groundwork for "The Rock" and the final
poems.

So, too, acceptance seems to have brought an end to the
"stubbornnesses and taciturn eras" to which he had confessed

only a few years earlier. Holly had married in 1944, and, a
year and a half after the birth of her son Peter in 1947, had
separated from her husband; and, as the *Letters* tell us, "although she did not return home to live, her apartment was on
Stevens' way home from the office and he often stopped by
after work. And on weekends she would visit her parents,
bringing her son with her. There was a feeling of family again."
Elsie gardened a great deal, and although he told one old
friend that he had done no gardening himself for years, he
was as much interested in the first snowdrops and crocuses
as he had ever been. The unsought honors increased and grew
more impressive: Wesleyan University and Bard College
awarded him honorary degrees, as did Harvard on the occasion of his fiftieth reunion, and Mount Holyoke, in 1951,
and Columbia, Yale, and the Hartt School of Music. He won
the Bollingen Prize in 1949. *The Auroras of Autumn* brought
him his first National Book Award—and he found, to his surprise and pleasure, that such honors "made quite as much of
a splash . . . in the office, which [was his] only milieu, as
any other." The interest in his work by young scholars led
him to hope that his poetry was "standing up under all this
scrutiny," despite the "excess, or rather, onesidedness," which
he thought often spoiled their efforts. He especially enjoyed
his exchanges with Sister M. Bernetta Quinn, whose essay on
"Metamorphosis in Wallace Stevens" pleased him because it
"paid attention to some of the smaller things—for instance the
Pastoral Nun . . . and the Yillow, Yillow etc. poem of disintegration . . ." even though, "after all, it [was] the subject of metamorphosis in general, and not in [himself] that
[was] the true subject." More and more, the scholarly questions concerned his "ideas." When, occasionally, the disagreement between him and his critics mattered to him, he tried
to spell out his objections, as he did to Robert Pack:

> That a man's work should remain indefinite is often
> intentional. For instance, in projecting a supreme
> fiction, I cannot imagine anything more fatal than to
> state it definitely and incautiously. For a long time,

> I have thought of adding other sections to the NOTES
> and one in particular: <u>It Must be Human.</u> But I
> think that it would be wrong not to leave well enough
> alone.

As his seventy-fifth birthday approached—and with it the
Festschriften in recognition of his contribution to modern
poetry, as well as the *Collected Poems* which were published
on the first of October 1954—he began to feel for the first
time that he was "pretty much at a standstill." He had resisted the idea of a collected volume, because it was "very
much like sweeping under the rug," and because he felt he
would have "difficulty in putting together another volume
of poems, as much as [he would have preferred] that to a
collection." Yet he had thirty-five poems, which he had written since *The Auroras of Autumn,* most of which he used
for the final section of the book. "It will, no doubt, be my
last book," he told Mrs. Church, "even though I shall probably go on writing cheerful poems on good days and cheerless
ones on bad days." He had wanted to call the final section
"Amber Umber," because he "liked the words even though
they sounded like Hopkins," and perhaps because they were
associated in his mind with the lines from the first poem of
"It Must Be Abstract," in the "Notes toward a Supreme Fiction," which meant so much to him, and which summed up
as well as any single passage in his work ever could, "the
drift of his ideas":

> How clean the sun when seen in its idea,
> Washed in the remotest cleanliness of a heaven
> That has expelled us and our images . . .
>
> The death of one god is the death of all.
> Let purple Phoebus lie in umber harvest,
> Let Phoebus slumber and die in autumn umber,
>
> Phoebus is dead, ephebe. But Phoebus was

> A name for something that never could be named.
> There was a project for the sun and is.
>
> There is a project for the sun. The sun
> Must bear no name, gold flourisher, but be
> In the difficulty of what it is to be.

But Richard Eberhart discovered the phrase in Christopher Fry's *Venus Observed;* and although Stevens had not read Fry (any more than he had read Hopkins), he understandably rejected it, just as he resigned himself to the title *Collected Poems* instead of "The Whole of Harmonium, Collected Poems of Wallace Stevens," which he had suggested "in an effort to get away from the customary sort of thing."

He continued to write, to create that world of his own which was, he now realized, shared by many more readers than he had thought possible, but as always with the persistent feeling that he commented on in a letter to Mrs. Church: "Curious—the satisfaction of this sort of thing, as if one fulfilled one's self and, in a general sort of way, had done something important—important to one's self." As he knew, "The feelings, the great source of poetry, [had become] largely the feeling of [and] desire to sit under the trees on a bench in the park." And although he could say, in "Long and Sluggish Lines,"

> It makes so little difference, at so much more
> Than seventy, where one looks, one has been there before. . . .

he could conclude

> The life of the poem in the mind has not yet begun.
>
> You were not born yet when the trees were crystal
> Nor are you now, in this wakefulness inside a sleep.

Slight, sometimes, as many of these last poems seem, their

transparence is a compensation for the lack of "transcendent forms"; and as if to bear out the conviction that in his own world he had become a native, he made of it "The Poem That Took the Place of a Mountain":

There it was, word for word,
The poem that took the place of a mountain.

He breathed its oxygen,
Even when the book lay turned in the dust of his table.

It reminded him how he had needed
A place to go to in his own direction,

How he had recomposed the pines,
Shifted the rocks and picked his way among clouds,

For the outlook that would be right,
Where he would be complete in an unexplained completion:

The exact rock where his inexactnesses
Would discover, at last, the view toward which they had
    edged,

Where he could lie and, gazing down at the sea,
Recognize his unique and solitary home.

"Unique and solitary," not only because he believed he had earned it or discovered it for himself, but also in recognition of its true value; the world had become more precious to him than ever. So, too, what had been in "An Ordinary Evening in New Haven" a "recent imagining of reality," became "like/A new knowledge of reality," in "Not Ideas about the Thing but the Thing Itself," the final poem of "The Rock," and the tailpiece of the *Collected Poems*. "The thing" was no more than "a bird's cry, at daylight or before/In the early March wind"; like the sun, it had come "from outside," from the actual world, the source of renewal and solace. He had come as close as he could to facing it literally and writing about it literally, with a respect for its uniqueness that was the equivalent of his sense of self. He had accomplished —after believing "most in the imagination for a long time and then, without reasoning about it," turning to "reality" and believing "in that alone"—the balance of imagination and reality as equals which would allow him to live in the worlds that both created; for both imagination and reality, he believed, "project themselves endlessly":

> That scrawny cry—it was
> A chorister whose c preceded the choir.
> It was part of the colossal sun,
>
> Surrounded by its choral rings,
> Still far away.

He no longer had to insist on the uniqueness of his perception of the world; master of its repetitions, he could appreciate his "unique and solitary home," valuing it for what it was as well as for what the imagination could make of it. "The plain sense of things" sufficed. The "commonplace" of a bird's scrawny cry or "the blank cold" became not only what he said of them, but part of what they were. In such poems, the poet seems to "confer his identity on the reader," and as Randall Jarrell has said of "To an Old Philosopher in Rome,"

> . . . it seems to us that we are feeling, as it is not often possible for us to feel, what it is to be human; the poem's composed, equable sorrow is a kind of celebration of our being, and is deeper sounding, satisfies more in us, than joy; we feel our own natures realized, so that when we read, near the end of the poem,

> It is a kind of total grandeur at the end

With every visible thing enlarged, and yet
No more than a bed, a chair and moving nuns . . .

Total grandeur of a total edifice
Chosen by an inquisitor of structures
For himself. He stops upon this threshold . . .

we feel that Santayana is Stevens, and Stevens ourselves—and that, stopping upon this threshold, we
are participating in the grandeur possible to man.

The triumph of "The Rock," in which this grandeur is
most fully sustained, lies also in the plainness of the speech,
though it would be wrong to think of plainness in Stevens
as one might think of it in another poet—Frost, or Wordsworth, for example; it is rather that the speech has become
so "authentic and fluent" that the poetry has reached that
"degree of perception at which what is real and what is
imagined are one: a state of clairvoyant observation accessible . . . to . . . the acutest poet," when, momentarily, at
least, "words of the world are the life of the world." He had
not foregone the unfamiliar for the familiar; but he had come
to see "the functions of every poet" not as "repeating what
has been said before, however skillfully he may be able to
do that," but as "[taking] his station in the midst of the circumstances in which people actually live and . . . [endeavor-
ing] to give them, as well as himself, the poetry that they
need in those very circumstances." How much the desire to
help his young Korean friend, Peter H. Lee, to whom these
words were written, and whose translations of Korean poetry
interested him enough to work a little with him, may have
contributed to the character of these late pieces, cannot be
measured; but the letters Stevens wrote him are among the
warmest and most considerate of the many composed between 1951 and 1955. Incalculable as such influences are to
the critic as well as the poet, they are somtimes more profound than those that seem most obvious.

What is obvious, in any case, is that he sometimes felt that "as one grows older, one's own poems begin to read like the poems of someone else," though he had given a lifetime to them, and to being himself; but in the end, they had succeeded, however "unbelievably irrelevant to the actual world" they seemed, in communicating not merely a sense of that self, but a magnanimous humanity, simply by having learned not to insist too much on its own importance. What he called reality and the actual world renewed itself as richly and as variously as his imagination. In a letter to Mrs. Church, he mentioned a "Sunday morning walk," when he "tried to pretend that everything in nature is artificial and that everything artificial is natural, as, for example, that the roses in Elizabeth Park are placed there daily by some lover of mankind and that Paris is an eruption of nature." But such "make-believe," which he once characterized as "the beginning of the poetic spirit" had its "difficulties," because of the Korean War, President Truman, "with his politician's desire for money and power," "disillusionment about the U. N.," and the threats to the freedom of imagination, which he so frequently identified with politics and politicians, not because they threatened his own well-being but because they made "a fortune out of life's poverty."

The threat grew increasingly remote, however, as the world which his poetry had created widened. Renato Poggioli, a distinguished Italian scholar at Harvard, who asked for a poem for *Inventario*, undertook a translation of "Sunday Morning," "The Man with the Blue Guitar," and several other poems, for Giulio Einaudi, the publisher; and for the volume, Stevens allowed his notes on "The Man with the Blue Guitar" to be printed in an appendix. Vincent Persichetti composed a song cycle on poems from *Harmonium;* John Gruen composed one on "Thirteen Ways of Looking at a Blackbird," and a Dutch composer, J. Wisse, completed a secular cantata on the same text. Although he refused Harvard's invitation to become the Charles Eliot Norton Professor of Poetry, he had begun to feel, as a friend said, "to live to be 75 is not, after all, a conspicuous achievement," and that "in the long run this remark makes everything seem normal, which is important as one grows older."

In January 1955, Mrs. Stevens suffered a stroke, which limited the poet's own activities, but not his correspondence nor the élan with which he had accepted the task of writing an introduction to the translation of the *Dialogues* of Paul Valéry for the Bollingen Edition of the complete works. The *Collected Poems* brought him his second National Book Award. By April, he could write to Mrs. Church that "We are trying to get back to our normal at home . . . and little by little as we regain confidence and return to our habits, we begin to seem like ourselves again, especially on the blessed days when the sun shines." Yet before the end of the month, he had himself been operated on for cancer. The disease had progressed too far to be cured; but he was not told this, and as he wrote to a friend, he expected "to be in good shape for the next twenty or thirty years." He received news of the award of the Pulitzer Prize at the hospital, but he was "convalescing," as he believed, by the middle of May, and catching up, however briefly, on his correspondence with Mrs. Church, Thomas McGreevy, and other friends. He received an honorary degree at Yale, which meant almost as much to him as his honorary degree from Harvard. For the Voice of America he wrote "Connecticut." What seems to have been his last poem derived from that piece, which was one of his few public utterances. Yet the two are really parts of a whole, giving the lie to the aphorism he had once recorded in the "Adagia": "In the sum of the parts there are only the parts." In these brief untitled lines, as in some earlier ones—"The Course of a Particular," "Farewell without a Guitar," "A Child Asleep in Its Own Life," "Of Mere Being," and the beautiful "Conversation with Three Women of New England"—there was a sense of finality and completion on a scale more modest than that of his greatest poems, but as moving as anything he ever wrote.

He returned to the office before the end of June, for a few

hours each day. There were no new poems. His condition worsened again quickly, and he died on August 2, 1955, just two months before his seventy-sixth birthday. Among his papers was a poem which had grown out of some lines he had inscribed in Herbert Weinstock's copy of *Transport to Summer* in 1947:

AS YOU LEAVE THE ROOM

You speak. You say: Today's character is not
A skeleton out of its cabinet. Nor am I.

That poem about the pineapple, the one
About the mind as never satisfied,

The one about the credible hero, the one
About summer, are not what skeletons think about.

I wonder, have I lived a skeleton's life,
As a disbeliever in reality,

A countryman of all the bones in the world?
Now, here, the snow I had forgotten becomes

Part of a major reality, part of
An appreciation of a reality

And thus an elevation, as if I left
With something I could touch, touch every way.

And yet nothing has been changed except what is
Unreal, as if nothing had been changed at all.

AFTERWORD

"WHAT CRITICISM wants poetry to be, and what poetry as a result wants consciously to be, it cannot be," Mark Van Doren has said; and his saying applies as directly to the poet's criticism of his own work as it does to the man who, not being a poet himself, would have poetry be what he believes it ought to be. In this respect, poetry must always resist the intelligence, that soft voice of the intellect which Stevens once warned against in "The Noble Rider and the Sound of Words." In his metaphor of "a violence from within that protects us from a violence without . . . the imagination pressing back against the pressure of reality," one senses not an irresistible force moving against an immovable object, but one force against another force; and in the great poems, which are the expression of both forces "as equals," the possibilities that life can be complete in itself seem momentarily realized. How often those possibilities occur seems to matter less than that they do occur. When they do, "our belief in the greatness of poetry [becomes] a vital part of its greatness, an implicit part of the belief of others in its greatness." Such an experience transcends all personality; but it is the greatest tribute to any poet that we recognize his words unmistakably and know them by his name. So it is with Wallace Stevens.

SELECTED BIBLIOGRAPHY

No BIBLIOGRAPHY of a poet who lends himself to as many interpretations and readings as Wallace Stevens can pretend to completeness; and as the books and monographs multiply, the task of selecting studies of value to the reader who is not a specialist or pleading some special cause becomes increasingly difficult. Most of the book-length studies are rewritings of doctoral dissertations, and suffer accordingly, although as time goes on, this state of affairs should improve. Moreover, much of the pioneering work had to be done without benefit or help of the *Letters*, and although Stevens himself approved of "pure explication," the endless exegesis and analysis of the poems which has occupied the attention of the majority of his critics is academic in the worst sense of that much abused word. The same must be said of the essays devoted to the "sources" of his ideas, as if, somehow, his poetry had to owe everything to his reading to be worthy of attention. He himself said, "While, of course, I come down from the past, the past is my own and not something marked Coleridge, Wordsworth, etc. I know of no one who has been particularly important to me. My reality-imagination complex is entirely my own even though I see it in others." And as Edmund Wilson pointed out in his essay on T. S. Eliot in *Axel's Castle*, at the rate that some critics go on, "we should have to read the whole of literature in order to appreciate a single book," al-

though these same critics fail "to supply us with a reason why
we should go to the trouble of doing so." This is not to say
that such studies do not have their uses; but "the fascination
of what's difficult" does little to make the poetry accessible
as the great humanity Stevens came to think it ought to be
"for all comers." Some of the most useful, readable, and valuable essays are relatively short; and I have noted a handful
of these, simply by the authors' names, which have been included in the three anthologies of Stevens criticism so far
published. Material for the specialist has been omitted. The
Wallace Stevens Checklist and Bibliography of Stevens Criticism
includes almost everything—books, articles, dissertations, reviews, dedicatory poems, and a few foreign sources—up to
1963. To pretend that much of this material is of real use or
permanent interest would be absurd. The same may be said
of a good deal that has appeared since 1963.

The text of the *Collected Poems, Opus Posthumous* (except
for "On Poetic Truth," mistakenly attributed to Stevens, but
actually excerpts from an essay of the same title, by R. D.
Lewis), and *The Necessary Angel* is, despite a few typographi-
cal errors, thoroughly reliable. Both the *Letters* and Robert
Buttel's *Wallace Stevens, The Making of Harmonium* contain
important juvenilia. The undergraduate poems, sketches, and
stories can be found in the *Harvard Advocate* and the *Harvard Monthly;* thirteen of the poems contributed to the *Advocate* were reprinted in *The Harvard Advocate Anthology,*
edited by Donald Hall (New York: Twayne, 1951). "Bowl, Cat
and Broomstick" was published in the *Quarterly Review of
Literature* (Summer, 1969). A few poems printed in *Others*
were not included in *Opus Posthumous.* Otherwise, the canon
is virtually complete.

The *Letters* are a rich and invaluable source of information
about Stevens the man and Stevens the poet. One hopes for
a somewhat less guarded edition later on, for a complete
journal, and perhaps a printing of the "June Books."

BOOKS OF POETRY AND PROSE

The Collected Poems of Wallace Stevens. New York: Alfred A. Knopf, 1954.

The Necessary Angel: Essays on Reality and the Imagination. New York: Alfred A. Knopf, 1951. (Vintage edition, 1966)

Opus Posthumous. Edited, with an Introduction, by Samuel French Morse. New York: Alfred A. Knopf, 1957. (Includes poems, plays, and prose)

Selected Poems. London: Faber & Faber, 1953. (The author's own selection, including "Notes toward a Supreme Fiction")

Poems by Wallace Stevens. Selected, with an Introduction, by Samuel French Morse. New York: Vintage Books, 1959.

LETTERS

Stevens, Holly, ed. *Letters of Wallace Stevens.* New York: Alfred A. Knopf, 1966.

CRITICISM

Borroff, Marie, ed. *Wallace Stevens: A Collection of Critical Essays.* Englewood Cliffs: Prentice-Hall, 1963. (Eleven essays by various critics, including Sister M. Bernetta Quinn, Ralph J. Mills, Jr., Roy Harvey Pearce, and Northrop Frye)

Brown, Ashley, and Robert S. Haller, eds. *The Achievement of Wallace Stevens.* Philadelphia: J. B. Lippincott, 1962. (Nineteen essays, 1920–1961, including notable pieces by Marianne Moore, Morton Dauwen Zabel, R. P. Blackmur, Howard Baker, Hi Simons, Randall Jarrell, Louis L. Martz, and Michel Benamou)

Buttel, Robert. *Wallace Stevens, The Making of Harmonium.* Princeton: Princeton University Press, 1967.

Doggett, Frank. *Stevens' Poetry of Thought.* Baltimore: Johns Hopkins Press, 1966.

Fuchs, Daniel. *The Comic Spirit of Wallace Stevens.* Durham: University of North Carolina Press, 1963.

Kermode, Frank. *Wallace Stevens.* Edinburgh: Oliver & Boyd, 1960; New York: Grove Press, 1961.

Pearce, Roy Harvey. *The Continuity of American Poetry.* Princeton: Princeton University Press, 1961.

Pearce, Roy Harvey, and J. Hillis Miller, eds. *The Act of the Mind: Essays on the Poetry of Wallace Stevens.* Baltimore:

Johns Hopkins Press, 1965. (Essays by twelve critics, including Bernard Heringman, Michel Benamou, Roy Harvey Pearce, J. Hillis Miller, Helen Hennessy Vendler, Denis Donoghue, and Joseph N. Riddel)

CONCORDANCE

Walsh, Thomas F. *Concordance to the Poetry of Wallace Stevens.* University Park: Pennsylvania State University Press, 1963.

BIBLIOGRAPHY

Bryer, Jackson, and Joseph N. Riddel. *Bibliography of Stevens Criticism.* Denver: Alan Swallow, 1963

Morse, Samuel French. *Wallace Stevens Checklist.* Denver: Alan Swallow, 1963.

INDEX

The Index is selective, and limited to titles by Stevens, references to his most intimate literary friends and correspondents or critics.